'Inspirational. Brave. Provoking. Costa bares his soul in the
journey of his life, and his story will challenge your own
vulnerabilities. *I Am Costa* is an extraordinary story that will
leave you inspired and your spirit rejuvenated.'

– Aki Anastasiou, media personality

'Brutally honest and courageous, this sincere account of the
Grecian soul in the diaspora, the Zorba madness in us all,
is at once entertaining and enlightening. It is The Catcher
in Johannesburg – a voice of a warrior, a survivor, a soldier.
Prescribe it for schools and let them hear him say,
I AM COSTA!'

*– Renos Spanoudes, award-winning theatre practitioner,
presenter and educator*

'Costa doesn't know how to give up ...'
– Lindsey Parry, Comrades Marathon coach

'I laughed, I cried. Everyone struggling with
addiction should read this book.'
– Kuli Roberts, TV host and producer

'Honest, captivating and heart-warming. Costa is a true
inspiration. An individual who triumphed over his circumstances
and personal demons to become the inspiration he is today.'
– Kate Murray, Olympic triathlete

I AM COSTA

FROM METH
TO MARATHONS

COSTA CARASTAVRAKIS

BOOK**STORM**

ISBN: 978-1-928257-58-5
e-ISBN: 978-1-928257-59-2

First edition, first impression 2019

Published by Bookstorm (Pty) Ltd
PO Box 4532
Northcliff 2115
Johannesburg
South Africa
www.bookstorm.co.za

Edited by Angela Voges
Proofread by Wesley Thompson
Cover design by mr design
Cover photograph by Gareth Jacobs / garethjacobs.com
Book design and typesetting by Triple M Design
Printed by ABC Press, Cape Town

For Dad, Mom and Sonia – thank you

For cousins Jonni and Michael
– for teaching us how to live

PROLOGUE

THIRTY-TWO YEARS OLD

'Man is a being in search of meaning.'
— PLATO

It was spring 2002, and there was a heady smell of jasmine in the air. It is always the first flower to bloom in spring in Johannesburg; on this lazy Saturday afternoon I took in a long, slow breath and filled my senses with its rich, sweet smell.

The sweetness reminded me of the honeysuckle bush we had when I was growing up in our family home in the 70s, a comforting smell of family love, carefree days and play. I loved flowers as a little boy and I particularly loved tasting the sweet nectar that dripped off them. The smell of jasmine took me right back to that era in my life.

I had taken the time to smell the flowers that day in spring because I was finally making time for myself and space for much-needed change in my life. I'd been feeling that I was losing myself. I was drinking a lot, fighting with a boyfriend I didn't even love, and working way too hard chasing a business goal I didn't even really believe in.

Who was I becoming, at 32?

Smart, energetic and charismatic, I had a lot of people in my life who loved me. I had trouble loving myself, however, and a friend recommended I do more of what they call 'inner work'. I had experienced the help of psychotherapy before, but felt like I needed something different. I wanted to try something new.

3

I had heard about Julia Cameron and her book *The Artist's Way* – a self-help book that positions itself as 'A Spiritual Path to Higher Creativity'. I had always considered myself a very creative person. I'd loved drama and school plays back in the day, and closely followed art and fashion and movies. By my early 30s, I felt I was so focused on business that I had forgotten that side of myself altogether. Julia's book was a well-structured 12-week course with techniques and daily exercises that were aimed at self-discovery. Like most things in my life, I approached this course passionately and devoted myself to unlocking all its coaching value.

A valuable part of the course was a daily activity I found helpful. It was called Morning Pages. Of these pages, Cameron says on her website: 'The bedrock tool of a creative recovery is a daily practice called Morning Pages … three pages of longhand, stream of consciousness writing done first thing in the morning. There is no wrong way to do Morning Pages – they are not about high art. They are not even "writing". They are about anything and everything that crosses your mind – and they are for your eyes only.'

Each morning I would wake up and 'dump' my thoughts, feelings and emotions onto the pages. I found them very therapeutic in that they did what she said they would do: 'provoke, clarify, comfort, cajole, prioritize, and synchronize the day at hand', and more. They became a place for me to feel emotions I hadn't felt in a long time. Most mornings, they were full of anger – anger at the world, my boyfriend, my business, the situation I was in, my excessive drinking.

As the weeks passed, the course suggested other creative exercises, and I took up photography. I would take myself on 'artist's dates' to disused factories to spend time playing with the light and dark of the old buildings and their broken equipment. I became obsessed with these derelict places, and the mystery and stories they held. A feeling of pain would often come over me after the photographic sessions, as they opened some soul space of my own that was derelict itself, abandoned and hurt.

I took to Julia's process of collaging in the form of vision or mood boards. This would often switch off my conscious brain – I would find images that felt right and paste them in any way I wanted to. It opened a space where I didn't judge what I picked or how I put the collage together – a free form of expression I felt I desperately needed. What I noticed being unlocked was texture, creativity and a new way for my soul to breathe (or, in most cases, vent).

Sometimes I would pick up a pen and write some creative passages. I even took to writing a few poems. The words would flow easily onto the page and over the weeks I kept coming back to an image of myself as a 12-year-old. I would often write poems from his perspective: lines about the music he loved, family moments, the games he played and the holidays he went on – soft, sweet times, from his perspective.

On the particular spring day when I smelled the jasmine and the association of the honeysuckle of my childhood came to mind, I was in a still frame of mind. Meditative, in fact; that day, it felt particularly peaceful and somewhat trancelike. My soul felt open. Like I was getting in touch with myself, my true nature.

I sat with my eyes closed and took in the smell. I let it swirl into my head and seep into the soul spaces and heart spaces that had opened in the past few weeks. I picked up a pen; the image of myself as a 12-year-old came to mind. I looked him in the eye and held his stare. He needed to speak to me. He needed to be heard.

He needed me to write the following one-line poem, a statement of what was going on inside me: 'There was once a 12-year-old boy who hanged himself.'

HERO'S JOURNEY

'Bravo, my boy.'
— MOM, ABOUT PRACTICALLY ANYTHING I DID

The start of an Olympic-distance triathlon! I'd grown to love triathlons, but one with the word 'Olympic' in its name stirred a particular emotion in me. I'm Greek, and proud of my heritage.

Here I was, standing at the start of a race that would test my all-round athletic ability, I'd have to swim 1 500 m, cycle 40 km and finish off with a 10-km run. You often hear people complain that they can do the swim and run, but they can't really cycle. Others love the cycle and the run, but can't swim. I roll my eyes. They're missing the point: triathlon is one discipline – it's all three activities, one after the other.

At 42, I was ready to start my first-ever Olympic-distance race in Germiston, east of Joburg.

Swimming cap, goggles: check.

Tyre pressure: check.

Helmet, glasses, gloves, cap, towel, water, nutrition … the list went on and on. Triathlon calls for lots of gear on race day.

But I was ready. I was so ready to take on this race. I had the one-piece suit on and looked like a real triathlete. I'd started doing triathlons a year before and was finally about to start an event at the pinnacle of my sport. A Greek, about to get all Olympic, following in the footsteps of my ancestors who had created the games to celebrate human endeavour and the perfection of the body and its ability to be pushed to the limit.

I was one of those men, now – fit, healthy and ready!

Who would have thought that 10 years ago I was writing poems about killing my 12-year-old self? That, soon after that poem, I would find myself in a deserted house in rural Mexico with a junkie, smoking crack cocaine for the first time? That, eight years before this race, I'd started a downward spiral that would bring me close to death two years later?

How does a downward spiral like this happen? Had the seeds been planted long ago?

ONE

My first day of school, 1976.

THE START

'Kali arxi, my boy!'
('Have a good start!' – a Greek saying to help boost the
confidence of anyone starting something new.)
— DAD

On my first day at school, in January 1976, I was wearing a slightly oversized white, short-sleeved, collared shirt and government-standard, grey school shorts. I had a grey cap with the name of my school on it. Bramley Primary School: a good public school in a middle-class, segregated white suburb in apartheid South Africa. A country ruled by an Afrikaner political elite that deemed me, as a white boy, superior to other races. The culture of our country was legislated segregation. Being white, I hardly got the short end of the stick when it came to this segregation, but the country's culture still made sure you knew when you were different. Starting school, I was about to begin experiencing my own 'kak' for being different.

I walked into the classroom. The only Greek boy in the class, I took my seat somewhere in the middle of the room. The teacher went around and asked each of us to stand up and say our full name. As is tradition in our culture, I was named after a Greek Orthodox saint. It was also, as is tradition, my grandfather's name (my parents chose my mother's side, as my sister, who was born before me, was named after our gran on my father's side). And even further to tradition, I was given a middle name.

My grandfather had two daughters only, and he wished for his family name to be carried on. So, it was decided that my middle name would not be a regular Greek boys' name, but rather his last name. This gave me a healthy, long, 34-letter name that was steeped in heritage and dripping with Greek tradition, like sticky baklava syrup.

Martin Sacks.

Lance Berks.

Jackie Plitt.

Then we came to me.

I stood up with a nervous grin and fiddled with my fingers. 'Constantinos Theologos Carastavrakis.'

The room erupted with laughter while I stood there, confused. It was my name. No one had ever laughed at my name. *Why would anyone ever laugh at someone's name?* I thought. I realised that day that perhaps it was something I needed to hide.

But how can you hide your name? Thankfully my shortened first name was Costa, and my middle name would never be used. But there was no hiding from Carastavrakis, which became the subject of a collection of jibes in my early school years. So many were thrown at me.

'Hey, Costa Carrot!'

This would morph into ridiculous iterations of, 'Hey, Carrots and Broccoli! Hey, Radish!'

I heard them all. 'Carrot' bothered me the most. I mean, of all the vegetables – we never cook with carrots in Greek cuisine! Such a bland vegetable. Later, a very English, private-school, close friend of mine – Tamsin – who couldn't say my name properly, called me Costa Taramasalata. That I could handle. Tarama is delicious, and as Greek as my dark-brown hair. But 'Carrot'?

My name – my primary identifier, something so integral to

who I was – was something that felt shameful to me, at the age of six. But it would not be the only source of shame, as I was about to discover at break times.

I soon realised that our school was pretty much divided into the blonde-haired kids and the darker-haired ones – the Gentiles with their fairer skin and the Jews with their darker complexions. Lunch break was a time when the divide became clear and groups were formed along these lines. I was faced with a problem, however. I was not blonde or fair, like most of the other Gentiles; as a dark-haired and darker-complexioned kid, I was also not Jewish. Where did I sit?

Well, I decided that on the fence was a good place to sit. There, I could try to dilute myself. Kind of fit in, and maybe not even be noticed. But it was difficult not to stand out, particularly at lunch time. Most kids would pull out their lunchboxes to reveal standard food, like jam or cheese-and-tomato sandwiches. Some of the fancy kids would pull out a chicken drumstick, and even some pre-packaged crackers or wrapped cheese slices.

I would sit with a very large plastic box that I feared opening most days.

Costa would not reveal a peanut-butter sandwich – instead, some days the box would open and release a blast of fermenting, sour feta cheese on top of aromatic meatballs – and, of course, some olives on the side.

'Oh, gross. What is that?'

'That stinks. Who eats that?'

These were common words I would hear while trying to sit in the middle, thinking I would not be noticed. Early lessons in being judged – judgement that led to my wanting to hide a piece of my cultural background. On many mornings, I would beg my grandmother just to make me something 'normal' to take to school. Something plain, that wouldn't attract attention.

'Please, Yiayia. Please can you make me peanut-butter sandwiches for school?'

But my pleas fell on deaf ears. '*Tha fas oti tha se thoso!*' she would shout, ordering me in Greek to eat whatever she gave me. And then she would send me off to school.

For us Greeks, food is everything. It plays an important role in everything we do.

When we are sick, we eat.

When we are happy or sad, we eat.

When the priest comes over to visit *after* dinner, we eat.

And we don't just eat. We eat Greek food. Thanks to my grandmother, the six-year-old version of me had been raised to think that Greek food was the only food of any delicious value.

'*Pou isouna?* (Where have you been all this time?)' my grandmother would shout. She and my grandfather had done what all good Greek grandparents do at the age of 70: they moved in with their children and took over the house. Well, my father remained head of the house, but my grandmother certainly became head of the kitchen. It made her feel useful in her old age, and gave her something to do. And control. She was a short, rotund, feisty Leo of a matriarch and when she shouted, we all listened.

'I was at a friend's house for lunch,' I would answer.

'Lunch? What lunch did they feed you? Come, sit down, I have prepared food for you.'

'But Yiayia, I've already eaten.'

'Phuh,' she huffed, and in her broken English said, 'Eaten? Is not food what the *xeni* eat.'

A *xeno* is a foreigner. Greeks refer to anyone who is not Greek as a foreigner, something that always baffled me as we were the

Yiayia, Sonia and the good little Greek boy.

immigrant culture in a new land. Our strong Greek culture, however, overrode such trivial facts, and we positioned ourselves as the dominant force – the obviously superior ones.

Particularly when it came to cuisine. My gran had a word for non-Greek people – *nero vrasti*, which means 'water-boiled'. And the water-boiled South Africans certainly didn't understand food, in my grandmother's eyes; all they knew was how to serve bland boiled food.

'Tzust sit and eeeeet,' she commanded in her super-thick Greek accent. '*This* is the real food!'

I would be served a full plate of food. I'm sure my gran meant well, and that there was a lot of truth in her thinking. My non-Greek friends *did* serve rather plain meals, but I would often dream of just some egg on toast for lunch. A piece of melted cheese on white bread. A little bit of Nutella on toast. Simple, everyday food that normal people ate. Instead, we were served rich meatballs in tomato relish with at least three vegetables and some boiled spinach drenched in olive oil.

'What about a Vienna sausage hot dog?' I once asked. I was severely reprimanded and reminded that hot dogs weren't even food.

I was also bored of the regularity of the flavours of Greek food, always more excited about food outside the house. Restaurant food takeaways or pre-packaged meals always excited me. When we would go out, I would always ask to eat some of it, sample the world outside our home, the different flavours that made up our modern South African melting pot of cultures. Italian pizza, Portuguese sausages, American hamburgers, English beef Wellington – yum! I would always get the classic response from my Greek grandmother.

'Why eat out, when we have food at home?'

The problem is, we always had food at home. A Greek family was always prepared for the possibility of visitors arriving unannounced. In the days before cellphones, you never knew which old aunty and her 32 friends would arrive in black. Or so my gran thought. So, eating out would never happen.

The thinking was ingrained: we were Greek, after all, and no one had food quite like ours. So, I was confused when I learnt at school that our food – the very traditional and distinct thing that nourished us so heartily – was something to be laughed at.

'Sis!' That word I would hear often. 'Can't you eat normal food like the rest of us?'

It made me want to reject being Greek, and food was one weapon I could use to communicate the conflict and confusion going on inside me. So, at home, I tried something: I refused food. I became notorious for simply not eating. I would sit for very long periods with a mouth full of food, refusing to swallow. I remember being forced to sit alone after everyone had finished, not allowed to leave the table without finishing everything on my plate. I would take a lot of it in my mouth, but I would compact it and keep it in one or both of my cheeks and refuse to swallow it. This earned me the name of 'dustbin'. I would keep it there for up to an hour, sometimes, until being threatened with a beating.

'Eat! Or I will hit you with the *koutala*.'

A *koutala* is the most feared item in a Greek household. It is known to have adjusted behaviour permanently in many a young Greek boy like me: a traditional weapon of sorts that not only cooks the food, but also disciplines anyone who won't listen to the one about to use it. I'm talking about the feared wooden spoon of the kitchen.

And in our family home, we had them in all sizes. The super-large one was only used to threaten and chase. Social Services would not have liked to see the damage it could cause a child. The smaller, lighter ones were often used, but a simple lesson in physics and velocity tells me that these would hit equally hard and inflict much the same pain as the large one. Particularly with a 70-kg, 4-ft 10-inch grandmother wielding it.

Food – feeding her family – was my grandmother's way of showing us love. She had lived through the war era in Greece, when food was scarce and people left due to famine. She was only doing what she knew best, given how she had been raised. She would sit next to me, very disturbed that I wasn't eating the fine Greek food she had prepared.

'Eat! Or I will ...' and as she'd say that I'd get a smack on the leg.

How strange, I think now, that the very implement that fed me is the one that would bite me. But I was defiant. I would not be forced to eat the food that caused ridicule daily outside the home. Perhaps if I denied the food, I could effect some kind of change and be given normal food to take to school. Food that would result in my being accepted and not judged.

This didn't seem to work. I needed to get smarter than the *koutala*. Many times, I was spared having to eat too much as I developed a naughty habit of hiding food in paper napkins and throwing it under the table to avoid eating it.

Withholding food was a strange habit that obviously concerned my parents. My mother may have let my grandmother rule the kitchen, but in all other matters – from school to social activities, church and homework – my mother was in charge. She and my father were very concerned with my slight appearance and, in desperation, they took me to a doctor. Upon examination the doctor thought my stomach may have been deformed, that I was born this way. 'Perhaps your son has a small stomach,' was his 70s medical diagnosis without a proper examination, but my parents' fears were calmed when the doctor suggested that this may just be a phase – a phase that remained really concerning for my family, as I was incredibly skinny as a boy.

'Skin and bones', as I was referred to. 'Toothpick' was another name I heard at school. My habit of refusing food had given me a body shape that made me even more ripe for ridicule. At six, I was not only the long-named Greek kid who ate strange food, but also super-skinny, bobble-headed and different-looking. Features that were, as I was reminded every single day, not accepted – and impossible to hide.

We lived in a largely Jewish area, and in our street most of our neighbours were Jewish. Some of us went to the same school. As a result, many of the mothers would form car pools. At one stage, we were five kids in the car pool. I was the youngest – and the only Greek and Gentile, of course.

All I wanted was to blend in a little. I welcomed anything that would sanitise my Greekness: surely, a 10-minute ride to school would not add to any discomfort I already endured at school. But on many mornings, any immigrant sanitisation I had the relief of attaining in the car pool would be lost the minute I got into the car.

'No way, what's that smell?' one of the guys would ask. 'Are you kidding me? Is that you, Costa? It *is* you!'

It was, indeed, me. Costa, the little Greek kid, would be woken up most mornings at 6:30. Yiayia would have been up since at least 5:00, and would be well on her way to preparing food for the family for the rest of the day. This almost always involved frying some onions and garlic first. From meatballs to moussaka to lamb, almost every dish started with frying up onions and garlic. Waking up in a house full of these smells, I wouldn't realise that they seeped into my school clothes and even my hair. While I'd sit swallowing my last spoonful of cornflakes, on many mornings the kitchen would be in full production all around me – a few dishes on the go, and the windows entirely steamed up.

These certainly are delicious smells when preparing for the great evening spread of a Greek dinner. Something you want to smell on another boy in a confined car on a winter's morning? Hell no!

I would sit in the car staring out the window, wanting to crawl into a hole. Long-name, weird-food, skinny Greek boy could now add 'onion-smelly' to his list of jibes.

The Greeks have been coming to South Africa for the past 100 years. With them came typical immigrant traits: they were hardworking, colourful people, full of entrepreneurial spirit, with a propensity to stand out among the local population. (Standing out was something I realised could get me into trouble. Being more Greek than necessary was something I wanted to avoid.)

They arrived in waves of immigration, and you could tell which wave someone came in on by two very distinct factors. The first was the accent with which they spoke. In the 70s, if your parents spoke with a very distinct and thick Greek accent, they had almost certainly arrived in the most recent wave of immigration in the 60s. Such parents spoke to their children only in Greek and shied away from conversation with many English speakers in the general public.

My father was the product of a much earlier wave of immigration – in the 40s, after the war – and my mother was born in Rhodesia, now Zimbabwe. As a result, they learnt to speak, read and write English from a young age at school, and spoke with a regular South African accent.

The second was the type of work they did. Those who had arrived most recently tended to have a lower education level and gravitated towards a type of business that became an institution of South African retail culture: the corner café. In South Africa, this was pronounced and sometimes spelled 'kafee'.

The corner café was a mom-and-pop-style shop that served as a general grocer or convenience market. It was characterised by its long trading hours – much longer than all other stores – a simple layout, all the basic convenience merchandise, and the *banko*. *Banko* is the Greek word for 'counter'. Behind it, the café owner would stand and serve all the customers. The *banko* is also the place where all the money changed hands and where many fortunes were made. It was also the place where many people were ripped off. Yes, many café owners were known for the ridiculous mark-ups on their prices; their unfair practices gave them a bad reputation. Not only would many café owners not speak to you in English, they would also charge you rapacious prices purely because they could – they knew no other stores would be open at certain times of the day.

As a result, I would overhear many people referring to café owners as those 'bloody Greeks', those 'rip-offs'. I had enough Greek, and its associated burden, going on for me; I was happy I didn't have to add this to the Greekness in my life. As a kid, I felt relieved that my parents didn't own a café. My father owned a Toyota dealership and garage with his brother. He worked hard – I was incredibly proud that he had a large business that supported our entire family so well. A business that was nothing like a less-sophisticated corner café.

Even better – my parents did not speak with a thick Greek accent. In fact, my mother didn't even have dark hair. She always wore it fiery red. These were small mercies for a little boy looking to fit in in any way possible. Small consolation in the swamp of judgement and jibes that immigrants endure at the hands of other kids at school. I could be perceived as 'less Greek' as a result … *Thank goodness*, I thought.

'Do you guys believe in God?' I'd be asked at school.

'Um, yes?' I would answer, confused about where that question would even come from.

'So, you guys have Christmas?'

'Um, yes, we do.'

'Then why don't you have Easter at the same time as everyone else?'

'Well, we do actually, once every four years, because we follow the Julian calendar, which is different from the Gregorian calendar. Easter falls on the first Sunday after the first full moon in the northern hemisphere's spring and because the Greeks …' Oh, whatever. Why did I even bother?

Of course, I believed in God, and yes, we were Christian. Easter jumped around a little here and there, so now I had yet another oddity, another quirky difference, to add to my list.

Religion was central to our family life. My mother and grandmother took on the role of spiritual teachers in our home and my mother would dutifully drive us to church on most Sundays. There was always prayer at the beginning of every meal and before bedtime.

My grandmother strongly believed that Satan needed to be banished from the house and her efforts to do so encompassed daily rituals of incense-burning and further prayer. Added to that, many icons were well placed around the house, along with crucifixes. (All this effort to banish Satan, when I knew exactly where to find him: in the kitchen drawer, in the shape of the *koutala*.)

My grandmother would also often fill the house with the gospel as spoken by wise clerics who, in the 70s, would record liturgies and other inspirational wisdoms on cassette tapes. She would play them in the living room on the large stereo, their high Greek incomprehensible to us. Bored out of our minds, we would nod our heads to feign some margin of understanding.

In 1977, my sister got her first piece of technology as a birthday present: a tape player. It was a small one with a built-in speaker, and it came with a special feature. It had that magic red button for recording. Finally, we could record music that was playing on the radio by holding the device right next to the radio speaker. A technological breakthrough for us, and one my sister could most definitely share with me as we both loved music and dancing.

Most importantly, we could play music we wanted. And we loved ABBA.

Well, that wasn't to be the case the day my sister woke up on her birthday to open her present. No: my grandmother thought it was important to give thanks, display gratitude for this gift and bless it by making the first tape ever to play on it one of her Greek religious cassettes.

'Voulez-Vous'? Hell no!

'I Have a Dream'? Yes, but not of hearing that old Greek priest blabbing on about *Satana* (Satan).

'Does Your Mother Know'? Yes, she approved the gift and had even bought us the ABBA tape a few months before!

I certainly wasn't going to be bragging to anyone at school about this moment. Being Greek was just too difficult to explain.

Sonia is my only sibling. She is three years older than me, a beautiful black-haired girl with large brown eyes that are so dark they are nearly black. As a young girl, she was energetic, fun and full of charisma. Chatty and spirited, she always had an opinion, and took control of most situations due to big-sister size and the fact that she was older than me.

I was fine with that, because she was just so much fun to be around. She was very playful, and incredibly resourceful as well. Together, we got creative. Playtime was always a big affair that took up many hours of the day. Often, it took up much space in the house too, across a few rooms. We cleverly purposed many props to assist us to create a world of play.

One such game was Office! Office! (It's strange how, when you play a game as a kid, naming it twice makes it something a little more official and important. Like Teacher! Teacher! or Dress up! Dress up!) Office! Office! would take ages to set up. We would collect stationery from around the house to make our office supplies, create entire workspaces with tables and chairs, fake files, the phone, drinking glasses, jugs, calculators, you name it. We would set up a smaller reception-like table a little in front of the larger boss's table. Once it was all set up, my sister would announce to me that I would be sitting at reception and she would be the boss.

Every time we played this game, she assumed this position. Something inside me knew it wasn't exactly fair to be the receptionist every time, but my sister was bossier than I was, and I would comply. *Well, that's what younger, smaller brothers do*, I thought. Besides, we had tons of fun so it didn't matter.

On many weekends, we had two of our first cousins to stay. They were originally from Malawi and were attending a boarding school in Johannesburg. We were all about the same age: Ginny was my age and Jonni was a year younger than me. Four cousins together on most weekends gave us glorious time to play and enjoy one another's company.

We were also the perfect troupe to make up the cast of another game we loved in those days: ABBA! ABBA!

It was always easy to figure out who would play whom. Jonni and I would play the two boys, and the two girls would play Frida and Agnetha. Being the oldest by three years, my sister would, of course, assume the lead role of the blonde singer Agnetha. We would choreograph dances and memorise the lyrics of *all* the songs. Hours would pass very easily in this game we enjoyed so much.

Being Greek, however, had its challenges for one of the songs we loved: 'Thank You for the Music'. 'I am the girl with …' the lyrics would go, and my sister would change the words to 'dark-brown hair'. Why not? As Greeks, we didn't have the 'golden hair' of the Swedish pop singer, so why not adapt? That's what immigrant cultures do. They adopt many new things where they live, and adapt where they can.

24

The Greek ABBA Troupe: me, Ginny, Sonia and Jonni.

But I knew I was more than just a backing band boy. I had a theatrical side that loved the limelight and being centre stage. Sometimes I even thought *I* was the blonde girl. In fact, I used to sing like I owned that role on occasion. Very quickly, my sister would smack the makeshift hairbrush microphone out of my hand.

'You can't sing. I do the singing. You play the guitar.'

I wasn't against doing the boys' thing, playing the guitar. I enjoyed a lot of things that boys enjoyed. I loved playing with cars and airplanes, and even had pictures of cars all over my bedroom walls, like all boys did. Having an older sister who was so entertaining, things were always more fun when we did them together, most often in her bedroom. Her room was a typical girl's room, filled with girly toys – and, of course, her collection of dolls. I loved Barbie and her elaborate fantasy world of glamour. I adored dressing her up, and my cars always came in handy for a ride out to an imaginary ball.

Playing like this felt easy and happy for me. I was quite a delicate, sweet-voiced and soft-spoken boy, and also quite effeminate.
Having an older sister was an absolute dream. We made perfect
playmates.

My sister did, however, push things a little too far. Once, she
dressed me in her life-sized doll's clothes. She wanted a playmate
and I was it! In the 70s, not many little boys would be seen dressed
in life-sized doll's clothes, but I was never told that it was wrong.
I was never made to feel like there was something wrong with
me: my sister loved me, and my parents allowed us to play freely.
I could be my sensitive and different self in our home. Looking
back, I see how lucky I was.

But when I went to school and looked around, I knew something wasn't quite right. I wasn't like all the other boys.

And the other boys obviously picked it up.

I had one of those little brown cardboard suitcases with metal
clasps and a standard brown plastic handle. It was the perfect
height to sit on, and sturdy enough to carry my weight at six
years old. One morning, in my first year at school, I was sitting
on it in the passage near the administration offices after break.
My head in my hands, I was sobbing my heart out.

I felt a warm hand on my shoulder and a voice asked, 'Are you
okay, boy?'

It was the headmaster himself. I couldn't answer him. I was
sobbing, trying to get the words out.

'She's ... not here ...' I finally managed to say.

'Who are you talking about?' he asked, his tone very soft and
supportive.

'My ... my sister, Sir,' I mumbled back. It being a large school, he
wouldn't have known who I was or that my sister was Sonia. Nor

would he know that, on that day, she was sick. On most days in my early schooling, I would go looking for her during break. She would always be happy to see me, and we would chat a little before I would go back to my side of the school and my class. It was a kind of check-in with her, my big sister, my playmate, my anchor at school.

Being social at school in that first year was difficult for me. Further to the lines of division I mentioned earlier, as most kids did, we'd also split into groups of girls and boys. I was super comfortable around the girls, mainly sitting and talking with them, having easily bonded with my sister. The boys, however, were a little more alien to me. The male cousins I grew up with were fun and easy to be with. I always felt normal around them just being my natural self. But at school these new boys had an aggression that scared me. So, I would try to sit with some of the girls.

Some boys made a mean comment the first time I did that. It made me feel bad, and a little ashamed. I picked up that I was doing something I wasn't supposed to do. So, in confusion, I would eat my lunch with a few of the girls, very quickly, and then go looking for my sister. She would make it feel better. I wouldn't have to be seen with the girls all through break, or try to be with the boys. Most of all, I wouldn't be alone. My sister would make me feel safe, loved and normal.

But not today. She was sick, and I was all alone at school. Break was over, and I was inconsolable. The headmaster lovingly took me by the hand and led me back to his office, where they called my mother. She came to fetch me – to take me home. Back to my sister, my family and my safety.

I just didn't feel safe at school like I did at home. Home was my safe zone. I could sit with whomever I wanted to sit with, play the way I wanted to play, sing how I wanted to sing, and feel free. My father, mother and grandparents were supportive of all the

Aunty Kiki and Uncle Chris's wedding. Dad, Mom, Sonia and I.

crazy, colourful displays my sister, cousins and I would put on.
My parents could obviously see I was different from most boys
but, at that young age, they never made an issue about it. I was
'seen' and allowed.

School was different. I was seen, but not for who I really was. In those early days, I heard words I could sense were not kind, but I didn't really know what they meant. I had never heard them before. Sissy, homo and paff were just a few.

It didn't take me long to make out what they meant and why they were directed at me. Hearing these words made me very quiet. I had no defences at school, other than my sister during break. I needed to find more tools.

I could have turned to my parents, but I thought about what the boys were saying – so strong were their views and feelings that I started to look at the world and see that I really was different. This kind of different was not normal. Was being a 'girly' boy something to be ashamed of? A dangerous sense of reality emerged – one in which I incorrectly started thinking that this shame was something my parents and family might not accept either.

So, I found the tool that would serve me so well as a kid and as an adult: I learnt to shut myself off as much as I could. First, I turned my smile off and, with it, my laugh. Then my personality. I would go into my own quiet little world. Being bullied immobilised me. I didn't know what to do. If I ignored all the jibes, I figured, they would bounce off me. The bullying short-circuited my brain. I became a very quiet boy, one who didn't even do much thinking. To block the pain, I would just switch off. Zone out. Daydream endlessly and become vacant.

Just empty.

THE FIRE INSIDE

Having built a strong wall of defence around myself, I learnt to cope. Quietly and on my own. As the years went by, you could say I got used to being bullied in the numb zone. I settled in.

I was still Costa, however – a little boy with a smile somewhere inside him. Someone who would dance all Sunday afternoon to the disco vinyls my father would play in the living room. A boy who entertained adults with jokes and funny skits. I could enjoy life, and even felt normal and loved – mainly at home, of course.

I was sure I could win the guys over at school. *That is all I need to do*, I thought. I was sure I could brave the wall I had built and climb over it. Assert myself, and be a little more like the rest of the boys. In my own way. It was worth a try. After all, I was sure I could do boys' things – like the rest of them.

In Grade 5 we were given a science project – to build something that could power a small motor and a light, using a regular AA battery. Science! Now that's a thing boys do well at. I knew exactly what I would build. Something the boys would understand. I would show them once and for all that I was a 'proper boy', just like them.

I started with a colour, going with a light-blue theme. I mean, blue is a boy's colour. I took a flat blue board and built a little fan that was powered by a single battery. Then I made a small box camera and attached a light to it, so that when you pushed a button the camera would make some light that worked like a crude flash. My idea was creative and grand, I thought. I loved it and I knew everyone would too. Particularly the boys. They would have new respect for me.

My title for the Grade 5 science project was a hint about where all my thinking had gone wrong and how all my endeavours were about to flop spectacularly.

It was 'Miss World Fashion Shoot'.

I took one of my sister's Barbie dolls and draped her in some blue silk. I made sure the silk matched the rest of the board beautifully. The fabric had to be a delicate silk, of course: I needed it to blow in the wind when the fan was connected to the battery. I had seen models posing for the camera in this way, and loved that dreamy look they got when their hair blew wildly. This was exactly the look I was going for when I positioned Barbie with her long, blonde locks on a small matching blue box, facing the camera, ready for her shoot.

I proudly presented my stylish and creative blue Miss World moment to my entire class, including all the boys.

It sealed my fate. The sniggers during the presentation were nothing compared to the comments to my face that followed.

'Homo boy.'

'Skinny paff. That's a girl's project.'

I would no longer have a chance to redeem myself. I was not like the others. The bullying would be ramped up a notch.

Unlike many South African Greek men, my father was very sporty. He didn't smoke or drink and was always a very healthy eater. He was in the minority among Greek men. He played tennis, too. He and my mother thought that a good way to get me

My glamorous mother with Yiayia, Sonia and me.

to integrate or socialise more could be through sports.

Being supportive parents, they allowed me to try them all. Growing up, I tried judo, karate, gymnastics, tennis, and the usual school swimming and running. My lack of hand–eye coordination meant I saw a ball where there wasn't one and almost always missed a tennis shot. My small frame and lack of muscle power meant I got flung around judo and karate dojos like a leaf in the wind. Gymnastics was where I had the most fun, but I was scared of flying and somersaults.

My sister used to dance flamenco. Each week, I would be taken along by my mother, who would sit and watch her; I was also made to wait around. I spent a lot of my time watching her, in fact. I loved the sound of the castanets and the dramatic poses, stances and steps. My sister was also beautiful to watch in her flared flamenco skirt.

At home, she would practise her steps. We would always end up fighting: I had a very annoying habit of watching her without her knowing. I had spent so much time at her classes that I had got to know many of her steps. I would often correct her when her steps were different from what her teacher had taught in class. That used to infuriate her.

Besides, what business did I have with flamenco dancing? Surely it was not for boys, I would often think.

There was one boy in the ballet class that my sister took. I really admired him. But it never occurred to me to ask if I could dance too. Even though another boy was doing ballet, being a flamenco dancer was just not something I thought was available to me. I'm sure if I'd asked my parents they would have let me. Was I too scared to ask them? Perhaps. Most of all, I felt the pressure of the whole world to do and be what regular boys did and were.

The one thing that all good Greek boys did learn, however, was Greek folk dancing. Thanks to my sister, I learnt all the folk dances and became a great Greek dancer.

Clear the dance floor! Here come the Carastavrakis kids.

We dominated. We were those perfect little Greek kids parents were so proud of. Dancing, carrying the tradition, flying the Greek flag high. My inner showman loved it too, and I really can dance. Once I learnt a dance and nailed it, I got it perfect every time. In terms of dance and masculinity, Greek folk dancing occupies a strange space that easily allows for boys to dance and not be judged in any way. Everyone saw my Greek dancing as fun, interesting and entertaining. Even the boys at school had nothing to say about it.

Weird: it was fine to dance like Greek men did, but this still didn't make me a man at school.

As a little boy, I would sometimes wake up with something very wet and warm around my pants and torso. Shock, confusion and tiredness would swirl in my head. *Why am I wet? What happened?* And strangely I would always fall right back to sleep.

The next phase was the horrible one. I would wake up a little while later in a cold, wet bed, always crying. It had happened again! I had wet my bed.

I knew what to do. I had done it so many times before; I would go to my sister's room and wake her up. 'I've made a wee in my bed, Sonia.'

'Okay,' she would calmly say, then not say another word. She would quietly and dutifully take me back to my room, dry me and make me change my clothes. I would then go back to her room with her and we'd fall asleep together in her single bed. Her compassion was immense, and she was always very nurturing in the moment. No bossing me around or older-sister judgements. She knew how uncomfortable it was for me and would only behave in a way that made me feel better.

The next morning, my father or mother would wake up and find us in bed together. If they were alarmed by the situation, they never let me feel it. The day would start like any other and I would come home to find my bed clean and dry. My parents never shamed me for wetting the bed. I was never told it was wrong or bad. I did have a sense, however, that it wasn't all good – something not to discuss with anyone outside the family.

One day, I heard that one of my cousins also wet his bed. That made two of us in the family. Both boys. Maybe this was something to accept? Perhaps it was okay? Of all the things I had to worry about, this was something I didn't need to give too much attention to. That is what I told myself.

But something was, indeed, up. My parents knew it. They had

a son who was not like all the other boys and, while I was charismatic and open at home, I didn't have many friends at school, my grades were average, I would wet my bed, and was often a very sombre child, which they could see.

Greek parents are notorious for having a tough approach to emotional support. Many are 'old school'; all good Greeks know there is a universal list of things one can do to 'fix' someone emotionally.

A trip to Greece is always on top of the list. The sun and sea and carefree Greek way have been known to fix many broken hearts or emotional situations. The *koutala* is the preferred weapon for beating away the sadness in some homes. Or call the priest! Some incense, black robes and a few lipstick-smudged icons open a spiritual pathway; being Greek Orthodox, we have direct access to the heavens above, of course. Food is easy to make and have shovelled down your throat. We are raised to know that a good meal can fix even a global depression. But the thought of a psychologist or similar kind of therapeutic support in the early 80s was most definitely not an avenue that Greek parents would pursue. *Therapia?* This was something for *xeni* and their strange ways of dealing with life.

I was lucky enough to have parents who saw the value in getting a professional to investigate my emotional state and see what could be done. A trip to Greece, a huge plate of food, and a blessing or beating was not needed. They wanted the best for me.

The therapist spent many hours with me and privately gave feedback to my parents, which they didn't divulge to me until many years later. She made some comments about my sexuality being in question. She also said that puberty would change things for me, and that being top of the food chain in my final primary school year would mean I would blossom.

When I was in my 20s my parents admitted to me that they were a bit shocked at the therapist's first conclusion. It was 1980 – I don't believe that regarding their 10-year-old son as gay was something they processed. Perhaps it was something they didn't want to look at or deal with. However, very soon after my consultation and assessment, the therapist 'ran off' with her friend and came out as lesbian.

Aha! Perhaps the therapist was just projecting her stuff onto me and our family. That, my mother admitted to me, gave my parents an opportunity to ignore the part of her assessment involving my sexuality. This was justifiable in those days. Besides, I was heading for my final year at primary school, and puberty, and things were about to change. I was beginning to find and stand up for myself.

But first: a trip to Greece.

For many 'immigrants' like me, going to the motherland for the first time is the most memorable event. It being my first time overseas made everything so thrilling for me. Everything was just so familiar, but still foreign: a strange space, where you feel welcomed and surrounded by so many people who are so similar to you, but in which you feel life is very different.

That holiday, I very carefully selected the clothes I would take with me. I loved clothes, and was always meticulous about what I wore and how I presented myself. I remember I had been given my first bottle of cologne, Tabac Original, which I safely packed in my first-ever toiletry bag.

I decided that holiday to wear a puka-shell necklace I had got in Durban on a previous holiday. These necklaces were made of small, round, white shells. Worn snugly around the neck by surfers, they caught on and became a big fad. I loved my necklace,

Sonia, me and THE necklace.

but was not allowed to wear it at school due to the strict uniform code. On holiday in Greece, however, it was different: summer sun, beach vibes and me!

I stood in the bathroom of the Olympic Airways 707, dabbed on a little of my Tabac Original and adjusted the necklace, so that the clasp would be at the back of my neck. Here I was, ready to experience my first overseas trip, in Greece.

'*Ti ine afto* (What is that)?' the fat little bushy-haired Greek boy in a scruffy T-shirt and dirty shorts asked later, pointing at my necklace. We met him and his group of friends on the *platia*, a small oasis of a play area that is common to Greek suburbs. With green trees and some shade, it was a place for kids to meet and play and old people to shout at them.

'*Ine yia koritsia* (It's for girls),' his friend remarked.

Oh dear, I thought. Here I was, thousands of miles away from my school-field bullies, having to face similar judgement. This, over a silly little necklace! I remember being very annoyed. My necklace was something many South African boys would wear – it never occurred to me that it would be judged for being too girly. Here, in a different culture, I was having to navigate their specific bias about what was acceptable to wear around the neck.

Of course, Greece has absolutely no surfing culture: their sea is so calm in most places that only the overweight grandfathers on their daily swim cause waves. There is not a single blonde-haired surfer in boardshorts to be seen among the Speedo-wearing dark-haired Greek boys. The little boys on the *platia* weren't listening to my Durban stories and decided my necklace was not for boys and that I should take it off.

Not on my holiday!

For the first time, I didn't care what 'the boys' thought. It was acceptable in my country and no bushy-haired Greek brat was going to make me remove it. Particularly one who clearly couldn't appreciate fashion.

It got mentioned so many times that holiday. Even the odd grandmother or neighbour would comment on it. We entered a monastery once; a nun made me take it off as she deemed it inappropriate for me to wear inside the Lord's house. I never knew dogma had a jewellery code as well – particularly one aimed at the adornment of a 12-year-old boy. That was the one time I did remove it, though: taking on the Big Man above was not something I felt strong enough to do.

With everyone else, I was defiant for the first time in my life – I wasn't going to take it off! Could it be that, because I was away from home, and leaving Greece anyway, I didn't care? If I were at home, would I have conformed? On this holiday, I wore the necklace proudly.

A tanned little South African Greek boy loaded with Tabac Original and a 'girls'' puka shell necklace, I'd profess: '*Etsi ime* (This is who I am).'

And, '*Ime o Costas* (I am Costa).'

I would say it over and over.

Final-year primary school, and the teachers must have seen something in me. Perhaps it was my impeccable manners, respectful way with adults, sense of duty and respect for the school. I was very much a good kid. Whatever it was, they saw me as responsible and capable enough to be elected as a prefect.

I was somebody, finally! More importantly for me that year, I was also chosen by the vice headmaster to be a mini city councillor. He was a gay man himself – we all knew that. (He used to talk about Greece and how much he loved his Mykonos holidays. Never married, in his late 40s, handsome, well-dressed and full of jokes? Yes, he was clearly gay!)

He must have looked at me, also, and thought what a good little ambassador I would make for the school. I think he saw in me a little boy who was well-spoken and charming, and who needed to be exposed to more of the world – to different people and experiences. I was now a sort of ambassador for my school on a council of city-wide schools.

It was like a United Nations for schools, although apartheid made sure it was white schools only. I was among my peers; everyone was bright, well-spoken and energetic. I had found a home. The runaway lesbian therapist was right; I flourished being recognised and respected.

I was elected to the position of President of the Mini City

Mr President of the Mini City Council,
with his vice principal on election night.

Council by popular vote by the rest of the kids. The Mini Mayor and the Deputy got the most votes. The person who received the third-highest number of votes was elected to the position of President, and the night I was chosen was an electric moment for me. I was called up to the stage and the official sash was placed on me. My parents, sister and grandparents were in the audience, shouting at the top of their voices. We were the loud, crazy Greek family in the middle of the hall! They were so proud of me.

After the ceremony, my father took us all out for dinner. My gran probably had food prepared at home, but such was the prestige of the moment that even her food couldn't match my parents' pride. Sorry, Yiayia.

As President I had many duties, but most of all I enjoyed

representing the council at formal meetings with dignitaries. It was 1982 and, on one tour of the city of Cape Town, I had to read out a poem as part of an official greeting at meetings with many South African government ministers. Most of them were architects and staunch proponents of the oppressive apartheid regime: Magnus Malan, Louis le Grange and Pik Botha, among others. As a 12-year-old boy who was a product of the South African education system, I had no idea what they stood for. I did, however, love the responsibility and limelight. It gave me a sense that I was valuable and worthy.

I was developing on two fronts, though. On one side, I was a maturing, growing, super-high-functioning boy. One who was getting more and more comfortable with the responsibility given to him, who many people took notice of and celebrated. But on the other front, I was a kid riddled with anxiety, confusion and unresolved pain.

'Stop it! People are staring,' my sister would say.

I would do it again.

'No, come on! Stop it.'

My sister was referring to a nervous tic I had picked up when I was about seven. I had a habit of flaring my nostrils. It was something I would do repeatedly for most of the day. I just woke up one day and started doing it. At first no one noticed, but after doing it all day for a few days my family did. On this occasion, we were out at a restaurant.

'But I'm hiding it, aren't I?' I put my hand over my nose, so no one could see.

'You definitely aren't!' my sister said, embarrassed that people were watching.

What I didn't realise was that, when I covered my nose, I

widened my eyes. I now looked like a boy in constant shock: mouth and nose covered, and wide, scary eyes.

Something interesting happened that day. I stopped flaring my nostrils but started widening my eyes instead. This began a new trend for me, for the next few years. I would sometimes substitute one tic for another. Motor tics, as they are called, can be suppressed at times, but sooner or later the discomfort gets too much and they start up again – with ferocity. Then, it feels like they need to make up for lost time.

I remember nothing more relieving than going into the toilet or my bedroom alone and letting all my tics run wild for a few minutes of delicious relief. It was my private fix of tic relief! My tics took on many forms. These forms never occurred at the same time, and some were more embarrassing than others. Widening my eyes moved on to blinking my eyes hard. This led to using the muscles of my head to move my ears ever so slightly, so that it felt like they were flapping. Short grunts out of my nostrils were the next socially embarrassing tic. Lifting my cheeks as if to pull a very quick, fake smile got me some strange looks, as it seemed like I was smiling at anyone who walked past me – at high speed. My next tic was a huge grimace followed by a short, involuntary shrug.

'Disgusting. You're gross,' my sister would say. And she was right: my most revolting habit had arrived. At first, I would spit tiny amounts in the direction of my feet. When it ran rampant, I would always check to see who was looking and spit in all directions. Sometimes, the further I spat, the greater the relief. The amount I would spit increased over time, particularly when I felt stressed. I then would spit large amounts of saliva into a piece of paper or hanky I would hold in my hand. The spit had to go somewhere.

I needed to do something about these tics. They were a reflex action that brought some temporary relief to the anxiety I felt inside. It was normal for my sister to notice and comment on them, but socially this was like adding a huge microscope to my life. *Look at me! I'm the weird one!* is what they signalled. I wanted them to go away, but just couldn't make them.

At the age of 12, I was about to discover something way more effective at relieving anxiety, and the tics that resulted, than anything else.

Before the age of 12, I'd never even seen anyone drunk.

My parents were simply not drinkers. We were that rare Greek family in which alcohol only came out a few times a year when we had special guests. I was never told it was right or wrong to drink. It just was something I noticed some adults did. It was a non-event; I never asked to have any, nor did I feel curious to try it.

Towards the end of my primary school years, one of my close friends, Alan, was to celebrate his bar mitzvah – the rite of passage when Jewish boys turn 13 and pass into manhood. Alan came from an affluent family: the event was a lavish affair held one Sunday afternoon. I was one of the few Gentile friends who had been invited, and I felt it was an honour to be there.

Everything was pretty much like my Greek world that day. The aunties were fat and had too much makeup on, there was way too much food, and the people were as loud as any Greeks could be. I was used to celebrations, and this looked and felt just like any Greek celebration. Each table had a few bottles of sparkling wine on it. During the speeches, most of them were opened and poured into glasses so we could toast young Alan and his passage into manhood.

I was thrilled to be included in this adult ritual. I was almost 13 and almost a man, too, I thought, so it felt right. That is the moment I remember taking my first sip of alcohol. It was sweet and sour at the same time. A very strange taste that bubbled all the way to the back of my mouth. I took a few sips with great excitement. It was one of those shallow, wide-mouthed glasses; I found myself easily taking a few more gulps.

At my table were a few of the kids I knew from primary school. We were not the cool kids. Alan was what you would call a book-worm, a nerd of sorts. The girls at the table were equally geeky. Conversation was a little stifled among us awkward ones. I saw them all toasting, but none of them had more than a few sips. The girls complained bitterly about how awful it tasted.

I had a bit of bravado in me and told them I would be the one to finish the whole glass first. That seemed to impress them all; I went on to fill the next glass to the brim.

'Look, I can drink another glass, too,' I said, and downed that second glass to a few giggles and clapping hands.

Two glasses down in a few minutes. At that age I was weedy and thin, a small 12-year-old. Not 10 minutes later I felt a strange sensation of numbness come over me. The room slowed, the noise got louder, and things got more colourful. Most of all, things felt happy. I was happy. I was funny, and life was funny.

This was a feeling I wanted more of, and my mind realised that it was instantly available in another glass. I had two more full glasses. Almost a full bottle in under 30 minutes.

That is when the details started fading. What I do remember is a friend of mine's mother, who was going to take us home. I remember telling my friend that I was really dizzy, and he made me swear not to tell his mom or let her see anything, or he could get into trouble himself. I remember her fetching us and taking us home on what felt like the bumpiest rollercoaster of my life. On long downhills, it felt like added G-force was dragging me further down into the car seat. I spoke very little in the back of the car, holding onto the door handle for dear life. She dropped me off at my home at the bottom of the driveway and drove off. I managed to stay still, and to turn around and wave goodbye while her car drove off.

We lived in a large house with a driveway that went up a panhandle for a full 100 m, up a slight hill. I now had to navigate that hill, which looked ten times longer, drunk for the first time at 12 years of age.

I stumbled into the kitchen, grateful to find my sister home alone. I fell onto the bench in the kitchen nook and blabbed the words, 'I'm drunk!'

Sonia looked shocked. No 15-year-old expects this scenario to unfold on a Sunday afternoon with her 12-year-old brother. Sonia was always very protective and motherly around me – but importantly, on this day she was also extremely resourceful and smart. She always had a plan and when I needed her most, she came through with flying colours.

I remember her saying that she had heard from one of our uncles that a cold shower and strong coffee are what treat drunkenness the best. She tried to pick me up. Together, we stumbled to the shower. She undressed me, leaving my socks and underwear on. We both started giggling uncontrollably at this unbelievable scene. She then placed me in the shower. I slid down the wall and sat on the floor, leaning back, looking up at the showerhead. Unannounced, she turned on the cold water, which hit my face and body with a shock I never expected. Then it started.

'Stop it!' I started to cry uncontrollably. I felt sorry for myself. 'Please stop it, Soniaaa!'

The humour and thrill of being drunk had been replaced with deep sadness, and remorse for what I had done. I was also incredibly confused: I had lost my bearings. This numbness was a new sensation to me. I'd been happy, numb and out of control all in one. But now the cold water had sobered me up enough to stand up in the shower. As soon as I did so, I felt the awful bile in the back of my throat. I was about to vomit. I reached for the shower door and took two steps to the toilet, where I deposited the large meal and four glasses of sparkling wine in one or two large expulsions. I sat on the floor with my head resting on the bowl, crying, bile dripping out of my nose. The 12-year-old President of the Johannesburg Mini City Council, drunk, semi-naked and vomiting into the toilet.

'Stop it now! Mom and Dad will be back soon. Come, have some coffee!'

My caring sister had made a strong black cup of coffee for me. I had never had coffee before either, but was ready to try anything to get this feeling to go away.

We sat there together quietly while I sipped the coffee. She never once judged or scolded me. I thanked her repeatedly in my teary way for bailing me out of this horrible situation. She had my back, I knew that for sure. This was going to be our secret.

The next day at school, word spread quickly that Costa had got drunk. No one had ever been drunk in our class – or spoken about it, at least. I was the first. My hangover on that Monday morning was overpowered by my sense of pride for being the first guy to have experienced something that only other older teens did. Only tough guys, older guys, had stories like mine. I now had credibility, I thought. Perhaps I was a bigger man than they'd thought. Perhaps now I'd be bullied less, respected more.

This was not the reason I'd had that first drink, nor did I have it knowing that I would find an escape to a happy world by doing so. It had happened quite by accident. But now, I had found what felt like freedom. I had earned some kind of weird respect, all in the form of a liquid escape. If I drank again, I would feel happy, fun and numb again. Of course, I was only looking at the good side of it. But life was suddenly good. I was no longer permanently at the awkward table. I was in with the older, popular crowd at school – the big guns.

But things were about to change dramatically. The pecking order was about to be reversed with the start of high school.

'Hey Caras!'

I hated that name. The guys at my new all-boys high school had shortened my surname. I know it made it easier to say my name, and that even a few of my family members would shorten it sometimes, but I never did. The bullying from my earlier years had made me hold onto it even more tightly: a justifiable defiance. It was my name, and it wasn't going to be shortened by anyone!

Well, maybe I'd allow it today. Just this once.

Actually, it was coming from a 1.8 m, well-built 17-year-old who went by the nickname of Molly, so I didn't have much of a choice. Molly was a derivative of some longer, very Italian surname, and our school was full of macho Italian, Portuguese and Lebanese types just like him. I was 13, one of a few Greeks, short, super skinny, and felt like the last person to be visited by puberty. A new uniform – one size too big, with wide-leg trousers and long blazer sleeves that hid my fists – completed my awkwardness.

'This yours?'

He was pointing to a piece of what looked like green snot that someone had wiped onto the wall.

Gross.

He was standing with a group of friends and they all burst out laughing.

'No!' I said, nervously. I mean, how could it be? I had just walked into the bathroom during break. Why was he asking me?

'Oh, I think you know it's yours,' he said, grabbing me by my collar and tie. 'Don't lie to me, Caras,' he said, pulling me to his face and staring me down, my throat constricted by his tight grip on my collar.

'I swear it wasn't me!' I barely got the words out; I was gasping for air. No time, of course, to correct him about my surname being Carastavrakis. 'Please, Molly, let me go!'

The irony of a female nickname for this tall, oaf of a man did not escape me. Not something to bring up right now, either.

From King of Primary School, I was now a bloody nobody again. At 13 years old, you were at the bottom of the food chain. The eagles that soared above were oversized men like Molly who could play, taunt, tease and bully as they wished. I screamed as he lifted me up by the neck and pinned me to the wall, where I was now at eye level with him.

'Well, let's see if you change your mind and own up,' he said as his friends giggled with him.

He held me up against the wall and continued to talk to his friends about other things, waiting for a response from me. Acting like I weighed nothing and looking the other way made him the cool, rough, strong Molly all of us new to high school had been warned about.

Defiant, I tried to breathe through his grip and say nothing, hoping he would get tired first and put me down. Who was I fooling? This man was not about to be shown up in front of his friends, and he had the strength and power to hold me up for at

Little Me in Big High School: 1983.

least the rest of the break period.

I gave in. 'Okay, okay, it was me. That snot is mine,' I lied.

I hit the floor as he instantly let go and, without even looking at me, walked the other way. His friends followed. He left me there without another word. I was the expendable part of his joke and my use was over.

Primary school had been bad enough, with only half the school being male and more prone to bullying me. High school was a concentration of testosterone raging in an all-boys environment. Shit!

I had found a way to numb my feelings before, and drinking could also be something to give me cool points. So it was at the very start of high school that the binge drinking started. It was cool to try the hardest liquor, neat, and in the biggest quantity. If you threw up, you accumulated more cool points with the guys; if you didn't get caught, you were even cooler. It was weekend fun, mostly with my cousins and full of rebellious energy.

Living in a country where liquor was easily accessible was a dream. We were never short of ways to scheme up getting drunk. Aunty Voula had a huge party at her lavish house, and there was an open bar. Easy. Let's sneak some glasses full of cane or Cinzano out of the bar area and drink in her dark driveway. Among the loud Greek music and dancing people, our shenanigans would go unnoticed. Looking sober was a little more difficult, but being young, I could always act tired and just sleep in the car.

A few times a year, our parents would throw a big party and stock up with tons of alcohol. When the party was over, my non-drinker parents would be stuck with a lot of leftover booze – stock we were only too happy to drink, as they never really knew how much they had left over in the first place. Besides, the stash would only be revisited the next time my dad had to stock up for a party, which would be months down the line – and many drunken, Saturday-night sessions with my cousins, playing pool on our table at home, later. (We had a huge house and the pool table was downstairs. We'd drink brazenly once we thought my parents had gone to sleep. They never caught us. Luckily for us, they were heavy sleepers.)

Once I'd started drinking, it was a matter of time before I added my next pleasure and new level of cool. I was 14 when the first proper long, slow puff of white smoke came out of my lungs. The numbness took over. A light-headedness that felt dreamy. A tingling down my fingers and a slight melting at my knees. A very long breath followed, and my eyes turned glassy. I was sitting at the back of our yard, leaning against a wall, my eyelids half shut. My head sank back a little.

Heroin?

No. I'd just had a drag of my first cigarette. I was hooked.

My curiosity about this burning stick, and the dragon smoke that came out your mouth, had finally got the better of me when I was about 10. My cousin and I tried the butt of a cigarette that someone had just put out. Of course, it went horribly wrong. I coughed for hours and didn't touch another one for a few years. Four years, to be exact – before someone showed me how to smoke properly.

Smoking cigarettes gave me a wonderful high. A fogginess that felt wonderful. Dreamy moments that lingered for a while. Finding that feeling was a life-changing moment. An easy mini-escape.

My father had been a big smoker, who'd quit when I was a year old. Smoking didn't happen at our house. But within a year or two, I was smoking every day. A wonderful bonus was that my tics had almost stopped entirely: one compulsion had been replaced by another.

It was a habit on which I prided myself. Smoking made me cool. I was even teaching others, like my cousins, how to smoke, paving their path to this liberating new way of life. The life of an adult.

By 16, I was smoking a pack of Marlboro Reds a day on a holiday in Greece.

Of course, I did it all behind my parents' backs. It was cool and rebellious, and I wanted more. Smoking had become an extension of myself. If you saw Costa, he'd be smoking. And smiling, trying to find his way in a macho world.

Poretti and Alfonso were Italians with Roman noses. Couthino was Portuguese, with wide nostrils. Diamandis and Lazaris?

Greek, with big noses. Cohen and Joffe had Jewish noses. And Backos and Rahme were Lebanese, also with big noses.

In our school, we had all the strange surnames of continental Europeans, and each nationality came with its signature nose. Finally, I wasn't the odd one out for being Greek. Greek was fine, at last. Phew. At least that box was ticked. But was I a *manly* Greek? The heat was on to prove it at an all-boys school; and proving myself as a 'man' to my peers needed some calculated moves. Why not try being good at what all boys do? Sport!

Rugby: Under-13F – wing position. The F was not for 'First team'. The F team came after the A, B, C, D and E teams and I was given the wing position in a hope that the ball *wouldn't* reach me. I couldn't have been moved further away from the ball and our school's strong rugby reputation. Just as well: the one time the ball did come down the line as far as me, I made sure I missed the catch. I didn't want to be tackled. Hell, no!

Water polo: two training sessions. Spent more time being dunked underwater than above the surface, and got tossed out of the selection process. Golf: swing after swing would do nothing to move the ball perched on its tee right in front of me. Cricket: I made the team! Yes, I was even in the photo line-up. I got to be there for every single home and away game. Except my bat was a pencil, and my role to be the scorer, who patiently recorded every ball and run. Running: this I had a bit of a knack for. It took effort, though, and with smoking taking up my lung capacity, I passed. A sport I'd show a very natural ability for many years later. Pass me a cigarette, though …

Being accepted as one of the boys was all I wanted. Doing it the regular guys' way was not working.

My voice was where I found I could be noticed, and hopefully accepted. I joined the debating team and showed myself as intelligent and unafraid. Being bright and having an opinion tended to shut some guys up. Perhaps I was just a little intimidating to the dumber ones?

Drama was where the chameleon in me strutted before the school, play after play, finding new ways to entertain. This was my way of winning over the guys!

'Caras, you're funny.' (Yes, the name had stuck.)

'Geez, you even lit up a cigarette on stage – you're so cool!'

'Dressed like a chick, you were hilarious last night.' Even in drag, my comedic talents were prized over any judgement about playing a girl. Awards and ovations were my scoreboard, and the tally was growing. Costa was getting noticed and even liked. Even the girls in town liked Caras!

'Caras, your sister's hot, hey.'

'Check your cousin, she's lank hot!'

'Geez, Caras. Who was that girl you kissed in the play?' (We had done a few joint productions with our sister all-girls school from a few blocks away.)

They were right. My sister was incredibly beautiful, as were the girl cousins I would bring to high school open dances. It was obvious I had something the other guys didn't have. I had a pull with the girls. Thanks to my sister, I knew exactly what to talk about with them. I made them feel comfortable. I was a magnet, when the other boys were awkward around them. I had cultivated charm with the ladies over the years, while the other boys fumbled. I was now a little cooler, and growing cooler still with each beautiful girl who would greet me by my name in front of all the other guys.

I was obsessed with beautiful girls, and none were more beautiful than models and pageant queens. The guys at school didn't know that my secret obsession would mean hours of research, reading every magazine or newspaper article or fact I could get my hands on about our local beauty queens. The more information, the better. I was (and still am) a wealth of facts surrounding them.

Miss South Africa 1978 was Margaret Gardiner who, at 18, won South Africa's first-ever Miss Universe title. None of it was televised, so we had to rely on newspaper reports to hear all about that life-changing night of hers. I was captivated. I closely followed each successive year, and invested hours in reviewing our national contestants and making my predictions.

In 1982, Odette Scrooby won. An 18-year-old girl from the little farming town of Brits was pushed into the limelight – in the same year I'd been thrust into Mini City Council fame. Perhaps she would shine even brighter than I did that year – but it was not to be. At the Miss Universe competition in Peru, she was robbed in what is still one of the biggest tragedies in the history of the pageant – well, to me, at least.

She entered the final night of the competition a clear favourite, with the highest average score from the preliminary rounds. She even got the highest swimsuit score. Tragedy struck in the final televised swimsuit round, where she was handed a terrible score and knocked out after the top-12 round. A very bland Miss Canada went on to win, and Odette came home with nothing. It was rumoured that politics were part of the decision, with one of the judges handing her a score of zero. The pageant organisers made the excuse that it was a technical glitch, which I didn't buy.

Her life-changing moment was shattered – but, as these things go, all my energy was put into our candidates in the years that followed. Each year, they renewed my hope that beauty would prevail over all else.

My high school highlight was Miss South Africa 1984, when

Crazy sibling fun.

we sent our beauty queen, Letitia Snyman, to Miss Universe, which was held in Miami. The outgoing Miss Universe was from New Zealand, and our queen was tipped to keep the title in the Southern Hemisphere. That year was one of the first times the event was shown on South African television. My sister and I recorded it on our Sony Betamax. The two-hour event would be one I would watch over 50 times that year alone. I could name the city that each contestant came from. I memorised the order in which the top ten and the top five were announced. Alas, Miss Greece didn't even place, a constant disappointment to us each time we watched. I even knew some of the scores the judges had given, particularly all the ones appointed to Miss South Africa in the different judging divisions. She won the evening gown segment in a red silk taffeta dress.

It came down to the final two: Miss South Africa and Miss Sweden.

Bob Barker – legendary host of Miss Universe in those days, and popular American game show host – said, 'Will you two ladies please stand here. I will read out the name of the first runner-up then Miss Universe – now the first runner-up is an important position because should for any reason Miss Universe not be able to fulfil her duties, the first runner-up will become Miss Universe. Are you ladies ready?'

My sister and I were holding hands and bouncing on the couch, teeth clenched. We knew who'd won, as the televised show had been broadcast a few days late. But that didn't kill our nerves or spirit. This was an international beauty pageant, and finally I was getting to watch one on our own TV set. Even better, our very own Letitia was about to experience a life-changing moment. A magical event!

I wonder what the boys at school would have thought if they'd seen me: Costa, happy to leave Caras and all those masks behind. Happy to escape to this wonderful world of glamour and beauty. A world where, in a split-second announcement, a girl's luck would change, along with her whole life.

I also wanted my life to change forever in a glamorous, sparkling moment.

Why?

So I could finally just be who I really was. Just be myself: Costa, a teenage boy who'd been sexually attracted to men for many years.

I'd dated a few girls in high school, but I knew I preferred boys. I just knew it. I related and connected to girls on many levels, but none of them gave me heart flutters like the crushes I had on the senior boys did. I would find myself staring at them at school. The tall ones with their dapper blazers and crew-cut hair. Fantasise about them, and want to kiss and hold them more than any of the girls I had on the go.

Did I understand it? Not really. What added to the confusion was the mixed views I was getting from the world around me.

On the one hand, I thought my urges for same-sex love were

wrong. The world told me they were wrong.

'Coffee, tea? Tea, coffee? *Koffie, tee? Tee, koffie?*'

A lean, tall, moustached man with neat brown hair would come past our seats on the plane. He was one of the men who wore the pale blue-grey South African Airways uniforms, and I remember looking at them with admiration. They all looked so handsome, and friendly. They had a dream job, flying all over the world and meeting all these incredible people. They were always congenial, elegant and polite as they swanned up and down the aisles making sure everyone was happy.

But '*koffie moffie*' and 'trolley dolly' were names I'd heard other boys use for them. Something was wrong, then. They were not normal men, and clearly not as acceptable as I thought. They were the flamboyant ones, a stereotype I noticed was shared among other men, particularly actors and musicians.

'Freddie Mercury is a faggot,' I remember one of my school friends saying. Queen were out in South Africa on tour and I was dying to go and see them. To me as a teen, he was one of the sexiest men I had ever seen.

But it was wrong, I would tell myself. Don't think like that.

At 13 and 16 years old I went to Mykonos in Greece, an island made famous in the late 70s by the Euro jet set who went there to live hedonistically – particularly gay men. Flamboyant, sexy men in beautiful clothes and way too much fragrance. Tanned asses on the beach, where men lay naked. I was fascinated, drawn to all of them. Their sexiness and their bravery. I wanted their life.

Then AIDS became news. They were the ones who had it. They were the bad ones who spread it. Gay was wrong. I can't think like that!

But this was the mid-80s. These were the gender-bending days of Boy George and his boyfriend, who went by the name of

Marilyn. 'Karma Chameleon', Culture Club's smash hit, made me feel the world was changing and that perhaps I had a place in it. Pete Burns was my obsession in those days, the lead singer of the huge pop band Dead or Alive. 'My heart goes bang bang bang bang', is what he sang, and that is exactly what seeing him would do to me. His long, jet-black, spiral-permed hair. His full makeup and over-the-top black outfits with huge frilly collars. Openly gay, these singers were top of the charts. At school, a boy could love them and have posters of them without being called gay. Somehow, this double standard was allowed.

Perhaps gay was okay?

'*Kita Yiayia – then nomizies ine koukla* (Look Yiayia, don't you think she's pretty?)' I'd say, pointing at Boy George on the TV.

'*Ine ligaki* (She is, a little),' she would answer. Got her again!

'*Ti saxlamares ine afta? Then ine sosto. O Theos tha tous timorisi* (What rubbish is this? It's not right. God will punish them),' she would say.

From Yiayia I learnt it was most definitely not okay.

From my parents, however, I got a different story. They gave me a sense that it wasn't bad. They had a few openly gay friends whose homes we would visit. One was a doctor who lived with his life partner. My sister and I noticed they shared one bed when we sneaked in our own private tour of their house.

How lucky that they could share a bed so openly!

I never once heard my parents make negative judgements about their gay friends and how they led their lives. (Sorry, Yiayia.) Was it actually okay, then? I was confused. Given what I saw at school and in society and the media around me, it was safer to think it wasn't.

I needed to try at least to keep up an appearance and try being

Traditional macho Greek dance: Zembekiko, *with glass of whisky.*

with a woman. Alcohol didn't help like I thought it would. It would have the opposite effect: it would make me very horny for men and give me the courage perhaps to take a risk one day. Maybe it would work? Maybe I could finally do what was most natural to me: be with another man. On the other hand, the alcohol made me sad. An emptiness would creep in – a hollow feeling that told me I was wrong to want a man. That I was not normal. Not accepted. A feeling that had to be dealt with.

How?

With more alcohol.

When I was 16, some of us got together and formed a small political group. We wanted to make a difference. We were anti-apartheid and knew change was needed. Our aim was to meet and discuss issues and try to get others to join so that our voices could grow. Young activists, full of hope.

At school, all we learnt about was white politics. Not once in any of the literature was the name Nelson Mandela or the ANC mentioned. You couldn't even get your hands on any books that discussed the broader politics of the day. We were hungry for the truth and got a taste of it the day one of our small group arranged for us to meet Helen Joseph in her home in Norwood in Johannesburg. There were about 15 of us and she had us over for tea one Saturday afternoon in 1986. Of course, we had to meet at her home because this petite, 81-year-old lady was a found-ing member of the Federation of South African Women and had been placed under house arrest for her political activity in fight-ing against the apartheid regime.

Exactly how dangerous did the apartheid government think our activity was? As we left her home we saw a police van out-side – someone must have tipped them off. Later that same year we let the group fizzle out in the fear of further police action. My family were not very happy either. Greeks didn't get politi-cal – that was something the liberal *Engelzi* (the English white South Africans) did – not the Greeks. This is a common Greek-immigrant type of thinking. We aren't really from here, and are mostly here for economic reasons – so, as long as the economy is okay, we are fine. Stay out of politics!

Politics were unavoidable, however, for all white South African families, as it was compulsory for their sons to do two years of military service. I was shit scared of this on two levels. I didn't want to fight for a fascist government I vehemently opposed, and submitting to a violent macho environment would mean hard-ship, and physical and emotional pain, that I could not bear to think about.

Sure, there were office jobs and chef jobs and ways to get

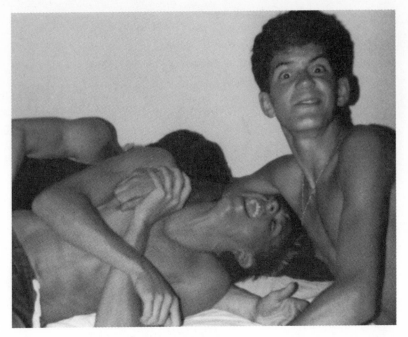

Matric fun.

around not being sent to the border to kill Angolan communists or innocent township students – but at skinny 16 I decided there was no way I would go to the army. Over the years, I became a fighter in my own way. I was learning how to use my assets to their fullest to get what I wanted. As a result, in my final school year my fellow scholars elected me as a prefect. Unlike in primary school, none of the teachers had a say. I was one of 12 selected by my peers to lead the school. Caras made sure that Costa was becoming a success, a somebody. Gone was the introverted 10-year-old with no friends who preferred to sit alone at school.

This somebody I was becoming even got chosen as a Rotary exchange student. On the entry forms we had to submit, I was totally honest, admitting that I drank alcohol and smoked. This backfired when my forms were mailed to a small town in Oklahoma, USA, and were returned, saying they weren't prepared to take me.

Two weeks before I was due to leave, I was the only one out of 85 scholars who still had no placement. To my relief, I was placed in Kansas, just north of Oklahoma – same kind of conservative state, but obviously my drinking and smoking claim didn't bother them.

My schooling was ending on a super-high note. I had the world at my feet. I was supported by my parents, who recognised that their son needed to spread his wings. I was a bundle of potential about to be released into the world.

I walked out of school on my last day, and the words that one of my teachers said to me will never leave me: 'Your life starts now, Costa!'

What better way to start it than with a drunken binge at our year-end bash at Emmarentia Dam?

Cheers!

TWO

THE USA: CLASS OF '88

'Just don't come back with an earring.'
— YIAYIA

Living in America had been a dream of mine since I was a little boy. I was about to learn what life outside my world looked like.

I had landed my big-city-boy ass in a super-conservative, rural, western Kansas town. So typical was this town that, in 1987, Tony Parker – an author from the UK – wanted to write a book on quintessential American small-town life. He took a map of the States and found the geographical centre – a little town called Smith Center (which made the *Guinness Book of Records* for having a barn that contains the world's biggest ball of twine; it's the size of a small house.) Parker then went to visit Smith Center, travelled to a few towns nearby and found my little town of Stockton, Kansas: population 1 500. I was going to live in the same kind of typical small American town that formed the basis of his book.

In Stockton, I was clearly an oddity. I was once introduced at a gathering as the guy whose grandparents were Greek, and who was born in South Africa to a father who sold Japanese cars.

'Huh?' said a new friend I made. He only had two questions for me: 'Why aren't you black?' and 'Do you wanna come for a smoke with me?'

A lot of the kids at my school hadn't ever left the state or even been on a plane. I looked like my new friend and smoked. That was good enough.

Arriving there, I became instantly famous. I made the local paper – the front-page feature article. Everybody heard about me and knew I had arrived, the skinny, fun-loving, smoking, easy-going African Greek.

My year there was an incredible part of my life. I learnt a lot of things – most of all, how to stand on my own two feet. Being away from your family at 18 is difficult at first. The calls home were weekly; sometimes only twice a month. This was the pre-fax era, so letters took forever. As a result, life just moved on without my family. I managed all my emotions, personal finances and social life alone.

I also created a wonderful new community of close friends, some of whom I even considered foster family. The warmth and love in western Kansas took the loneliness away. I was the toast of the town and my impeccable manners were called upon on most weeks when I was invited to do a talk on my home country and myself. So popular was I that I had at least one speaking engagement a week in the first few months. I talked at all sorts of gatherings, from the Veterans of Foreign Wars society to the Future Farmers of America group and the Local Nurses Committee. I came alive and out of my shell. I was really coming into my own, about to transition into adulthood.

Humility was handed to me in heavy doses when I accepted a house-cleaning job from one of my English teachers. She had a few cats and some rather relaxed hygiene habits. Here I was, a guy who'd had a domestic worker cleaning up after him all his life, cleaning other people's houses.

My next job was cleaning toilets and washing dishes at the local country club. Thankfully I was given one clean job, which

Howdy Cowboy: Stockton, Kansas, 1988.

involved the setting up and maintenance of the salad bar. I worked this job for many months and came to enjoy the challenge of being the best I could at it. I had this drive in me to be impeccable in everything I did. That salad bar was always freshly stocked, and the toilets sparkled!

Best of all, these jobs gave me some money – money I could use to have fun, fun, and fun. What do seniors do in a small school in western Kansas on weekends? The movie *Footloose* may give you a good idea of the kind of conservative town Stockton was. In fact, in two of my host families, one of the parents was a priest. Friday was football and Sunday morning was church. The rest of the weekend was heavy metal music and alcohol.

I was already a serious smoker at 17, but in the US you needed to be 18 to buy cigarettes. Something alien to me, because in my home country there wasn't a similar age requirement. Worse, you needed to be 21 to buy alcohol. *Bloody strange*, I thought. It put a pesky brake on my drinking for a while. You could drive at 16; vote, get married and be killed in a war at 18, but only buy a beer legally three years later. I had to get around this and I did.

Mixed with a heavy dose of open wheat plains, western Kansas boredom led to a life of wild and irresponsible weekend behaviour. The most common thing for us to do was fill up a car with loads of alcohol and drive up and down the main road smoking and drinking until somebody heard or found a party. How much alcohol? Towards the end of my year, it was easily a 12-pack of Old Milwaukee light beer – in the long can. Yes, 12 beers in a single night. Easy! This was always accompanied by at least a packet of cigarettes. In those days, it was Marlboro Lights Menthol 100s.

Nothing I did, however, was approved by the boys. There were only 70 boys in the whole high school, making me a clear threat. They didn't need another guy to impress, court or date their limited stock of girls in the school.

They all said I dressed funny in my large *Cosby Show*-style cable-knit jerseys, moccasins and tracksuit pants, all bought at the high-end mall back home in Sandton. I mean, we dressed up where I came from. In Stockton, guys wore tractor caps, and some even cowboy boots. Me? Slick crew-cut hair with white lace-up shoes – laces on the side, of course. This had to change if I wanted to fit in.

'Foreign Exchange Fago' was on a note stuck to my locker once. 'Costa' was carved into the desk where I sat in Biology class, which got me suspended. I didn't care as much as I thought I would. The girls loved me; I had a huge group of girls I hung out with. They all had cars and tons of time for me.

'Costaaa!' they would call, hooting outside the house I was staying in. 'Let's go!' And we'd drive off on a Saturday night for some fun. Driving up and down looking for fun often got us into trouble. Luckily, the girls would always charm the cops and we'd get away with it.

Popularity with the girls meant I had many of them make serious advances on me. One girl I actually fell for – a beautiful (of course), exceptionally intelligent, gifted pianist with an infectious giggle and chatty way. But I knew deep down it wasn't girls I liked … it was guys. But when you have enough people around you, affirming you, and enough alcohol, and enough loud music and new experiences that are there to be enjoyed, you push those thoughts back. Rather, I pushed them down; I washed down the confusing feelings, the strange emotions that I just didn't understand, with crate after crate of beer.

In Kansas, I added another addiction to my growing list. But this one was a socially acceptable addition in America: food.

It was the land of *everything*. Nothing was cooler to me than the food Americans ate. In the movies we watched and magazines and *Archie* comics we read, we would see McDonald's, Hostess Twinkie Pies, Dr Pepper and Burger King. With South Africa being an isolated country, particularly before the age of globalisation, we had very little of what the rest of the world had. I arrived to an extravagant buffet of everything I wanted to experience in terms of food. I ploughed through all-you-can-eat buffets at Circus Circus in Las Vegas, McDonald's Big Mac meals, extra-large pizzas from Pizza Hut, and more. Grocery shopping was a new kind of exposure to exciting packaged and processed food.

Our little town had a single grocery store with at least half an aisle dedicated to cereal. There was hardly a fresh food section to speak of; the new women in my life included Betty Crocker. My addictive nature was in ecstasy. I pushed my feelings down not only with alcohol and cigarettes, but now also with food.

Sugar, sugar and more sugar. It was in everything I liked, and I couldn't get enough. My host families had a tricky time getting used to me, as I would often finish most of the food in their refrigerators. I discovered decadent Cool Whip cream in a litre container. I used to love finishing one, on my own, in one sitting. Those 12 ice cream pops in the freezer? An easy Saturday night treat. Yes, all 12. I particularly remember Jolt Cola, with the description on the can that said 'All the sugar and twice the caffeine'. Yes please! The best part of it all was that I remained super skinny. I could eat whatever I wanted and nothing would stick to my frame. From having refused food as a kid, I was now referred to as the 'human trash can' for another reason.

On weekends, the rock music was hard and the drinking harder. Sunday morning neck pain from headbanging and a massive hangover were signs of a good weekend.

We were drunk and cool. Invincible.

My year as an exchange student ended with a decision to go to university. I was accepted to do a marketing degree at the University of Cape Town (UCT). Bonus: I would defer the army for another four years.

Sitting on the plane that had just landed back home, I was the very last one to get off. A cabin attendant came up to me to coax me off. I was still deep in thought. I had discovered so much about myself and life. I'd been living it to the full, achieving so many great things. Was I comfortable with who I really was? On some levels, yes. Caras had vanished, and Costa was beginning to flourish.

I was still a little drunk, the plane's free alcohol swirling inside me.

I had to pull myself together. Time to put on a smile and step off the plane into the next chapter of my life.

UNIVERSITY DAYS AND HAZE

'Sundays are for church, my boy.'
— YIAYIA

I was sitting on the beach in Cape Town in 1992, my final year at university.

It was 6:00 on a Sunday and the sun was coming up.

My date was sitting on the pavement outside my car. She was a little cold and still wearing her black velvet cape. I was in my tux jacket but couldn't find my bowtie anywhere. We looked like two vampires on the side of the road: tired, pale-faced, all in black. Neither of us could get into the car because I'd snapped my car key off in the lock.

We were alone with only the odd car, morning cyclist or runner passing us.

The night had started at a huge black-tie function, another all-nighter. At university, there was always a party. Always someone to drink with, and always an event of some sort. Sundowners on the legendary Llandudno Beach. Boozy lunches at the newly opened V&A Waterfront. Happy hour at the infamous Pig and Whistle in Rondebosch. More house parties than you could count.

'What are we going to do? Do you know where your spare key is? I mean, you need to take me home ... Do you have any money left?'

'I have enough for a taxi to town,' I said.

Why, why, why had I insisted on yet another all-nighter and

seeing the sunrise from the beach before going home? Why hadn't we just left earlier?

'Let's do this!' I reached out my hand and pulled her up.

She was giggling, thankfully, starting to find this funny. We were both still drunk. I lifted my arm and hailed one of the local 16-seater taxis that transported most of the city's workers. Black velvet capes and tuxedos don't often travel in these taxis; we had little choice but to smile as the other passengers laughed at us and asked us a ton of questions. In apartheid South Africa, not many white people used these taxis, and we were a novelty. It made us feel better.

Our hopes of getting home were soon dashed when the taxi ride ended outside Cape Town's main train station. It was about 9:00.

'Now what?' my date asked, her heels starting to hurt her. It was hot. She had the velvet cape over one arm and was wearing a tight-fitting, short black number. A strikingly beautiful girl with long black hair. Most of the men were staring at her.

'Sexy lady,' one called.

Ordinarily that would fill me with pride: another man noticing my girl. Another man seeing me as straight and worthy of being a man, all because I had a hot lady next to me. This time, it was different. We were hungover and shaky, and I was concerned about the safety of my date. We had to get out of there.

I started to feel ashamed about the situation. Here I was, about to graduate in a few months, dressed smartly, a bright guy standing on the side of the road, still drunk from the night before. I was no better than the guy sleeping on the sidewalk.

The shame deepened when I realised I was putting my date through this as well. No lady deserved to be treated like this.

'Let's hitch a ride home. It will be safe. It's our only chance of getting home now we've no money left,' I explained to her. She was up for it. Well, she didn't have much of a choice.

I spared her the humiliation and put my own thumb out. We waited for about 30 minutes, but no one would stop. Perhaps it was the couple standing there, out of context, that frightened people.

'We look like a Halloween party threw us up,' my date joked. At least she could find some humour in the situation.

Then, a large car stopped a few metres ahead of us. We galloped over and I opened the door. 'Rondebosch, southern suburbs?' I asked.

'Yes, yes, get in, Costa,' said the driver.

Oh shit!

'Oh, hi George! Hi, Mrs M. Thank you for stopping.'

There was a deathly silence as we piled into the back of the car. I think our smell filled the space. Mrs M was not impressed that her son George had stopped to give us a lift.

George was a Greek friend of mine from university. His mother was a meticulous woman who worked at a prestigious beauty counter in one of Cape Town's department stores. She was a stoical woman whom everybody in the Greek community respected highly.

Her lips pursed. 'You drop me off at church first, George.'

Of course! Greek church! It was a Sunday morning. That's what Greeks did!

I was instantly conscious of how much we stank of alcohol and smoke. We were coming home as everyone else was heading out to church or the beach.

George was kind enough to ask about university and make small talk, and I made certain to pepper my answers with Greek words to impress Mrs M with my intelligence. Saving face is a

Greek thing. Being a well-behaved, upstanding member of the community is imperative. Thankfully, not many people knew my family. Our family name would remain intact with this incident. Mine, however, was in the mud.

I was well liked by most of the Greek community. I would be invited to dinners all the time at my friends' houses, and always charmed their parents. I was what my uncle once said was 'a good kid', and also a bit of a catch. I was a new Greek man in a city with few Greek marriage potential options. Word was I'd come from a 'very good family' and had a 'bright future with a good university degree in the making'. I was also head of the social committee of the Greek Students' Association – of course.

I had got into a bit of trouble now and again in front of Greeks. Once, I'd been caught smuggling a bottle of whisky out of the bar at Dimitri Papadopoulos's 21st birthday. But I could talk and laugh my way out of most of these situations. On this day, however, the look of disgust on Mrs M's face was one only a Greek mother could have given me. I was grateful that my own mother never got to experience me in this state. I had always managed to hide all this from my parents. I didn't live near home, which helped a lot. Alone in my own city, I could forge my own identity and hide anything bad that I didn't want my family to know.

Church! Oh dear, there it was. We had stopped in front of it for Mrs M to get out.

I sprang out the car and opened the door for her. She got out, greeted her son and walked off. She totally ignored me, which deepened my shame. I quickly got in the car and off we went.

Phew, I'd slipped away without seeing anyone I knew.

But how many of these moments was I in for in this life? Dodging and diving and drinking and dancing? Moments like these were becoming a lifestyle. And the truth was that I was in for a whole lot more in the next decade. I was not going to cut down on my drinking, and was going to take all the risks that came with it. In fact, I threw myself into it even harder.

One of the biggest drinking events was always a full week of intervarsity rugby when we would take on our arch-nemesis, Stellenbosch University. In a drunken dare I dashed across the rugby field, only to be tackled by security and scolded by the ref in front of thousands of spectators. I was drunk, and a university student – that's what we did, I thought.

Except I was the one doing it a little more than most.

Despite my heavy drinking, I was a diligent student. My grades were important to me and I was enjoying my degree. I was lucky to have my parents pay for everything. I wanted to respect that and succeed. Many other students skipped lectures, but I always panicked at the thought of missing out on anything and getting left behind. I also saw it as a slap in the face of my parents, who were paying for my education. As I often used to say, missing lectures was like paying for a movie and not going. With this atti-tude, I never missed a class unless I was physically sick.

Often, I was very hungover when I made it up to the beauti-ful campus. But being on campus was a chance to be social and being social was something I was very good at. I didn't want to miss out on any news and events. I needed to be at the centre of it all.

I managed to pace myself very well and stayed in the top 25 per cent of the class in most subjects. I did this by working hard. I would lock myself up in my flat, chain smoking for days before exams, to get these results. This kind of discipline was easy for me to maintain.

Then I would give myself a huge reward.

Sometimes, we started the study week with a big night out.

Jonni and me in Mykonos.

*Gordon, my close
university friend, and
myself, 1991.*

Then we took a mid-week big night out. Then a post-first-exam
big night out. And so on. The joke among my friends was that
I was either behind a desk studying hard, or out drinking and
dancing. At least I was balancing things out: the good guy with
the bad brat. But flippant analogies like these were about to look
trivial in light of a harrowing experience at gunpoint.

HIJACKED

'Lock your doors.'
— YIAYIA

South Africa in the transition from apartheid to democracy had a lot of political unrest, and the effects of crime on middle-class white people were increasing. No way you could walk alone in a dodgy part of town. Most of the crime was in crazy Joburg. Provincial Cape Town was much safer and was nothing like the tourist mecca it is today. Violent crime happened mostly in the poorer areas due to gang violence.

UCT is in the safe neighbourhood of Rondebosch. Its safety was guaranteed because there were always so many students around. There was always somebody watching, some couple snogging on the lawns, and criminals certainly had a tough time getting away with things. We even had our own small security force that patrolled campus, keeping a beady eye on things. In this super-safe environment, I was sitting in my car at 19:30 outside Tugwell Hall women's residence to fetch my friend Carin. It was the beginning of study week before final exams in my final year, and we'd decided to go and have some fun before attacking the books. I was prepared and confident. I just needed one last big push to get over the finish line.

But first, a cocktail and a night out.

I waited. There were no cell phones in those days. Earlier that day, we'd planned for that time. She was always late, though, so I sat in the car and lit a cigarette. Ten minutes passed and still no Carin.

Do I go and call her? Nah, she'll be out in a flash. Let's have another smoke.

'Get in the back! Get in the back!' a gruff voice said nervously.

'Huh? What?' What was going on? I turned to the right and was facing a gun. At that moment the back door on the right opened and a man got into the car.

'Get in the back!' He was shouting now.

How could I? There was someone to my right with a gun and no way out. Just then, the guy in the back pulled me hard by my shirt.

'Get over the seat.' He pulled hard around my neck, dragging me back through the gap in the seats. I was contorted and pulled backwards until I was sitting upright behind the driver's seat. By now the gunman had got in. He passed the gun to the guy in the back with me, who put it against my temple.

You don't realise how cold and heavy a gun is until it's resting on your temple.

I froze. My mouth dried instantly. There was a huge rush of blood to my heart. A pounding in my ears. What was going on?

He started the car and we drove off. I had a gun to my temple and my mind pictured my head being blown off. I saw blood and brains on the window and back of the front seat. I replayed that scene, over and over. *Get it over with*, I thought. *Make this end.*

We turned off campus and headed to the main road.

'Please let me go.' I found the courage to speak. 'Please. You can have my car.'

Suddenly a yellow-and-blue police van turned into the road ahead of us.

'Get down, get down!' He smacked the back of my head with

his free hand, then pushed my face onto my knees uncomfortably.

Oh thank God, I thought as he moved the gun from the side of my head to my thigh. *If he has to shoot, at most I'll lose my leg. That's okay*, I thought. *That's okay.*

I couldn't see where we were but within a few hundred metres I heard the indicator tick. He was turning right. That meant only one thing. He was taking the highway.

In the direction we were driving in, the highway led away from the city towards the poorer areas, the townships and squatter camps of Cape Town. Immediately I knew that they were not about to drop me off.

'Please let me go.'

Pleading for your life at the hands of another is hard to describe. Somebody else has the power to end your life and you only have one tool when there is a gun pointed at you – to beg.

'I promise, I won't call the police. I will go home. I need to study. I won't call anyone. Please let me go. Here, I have my gold cross and chain for you.' I reached for my neck to take it off, the cross given to me by my godparents when I was christened. On it was my full name, Constantinos, and my date of birth. The cross hung on a solid-gold chain.

These irreplaceable items meant nothing when compared to my life.

They started arguing among themselves. What were they saying?

The driver slammed on brakes.

'Get out!' The man beside me opened the door facing the highway and pushed me onto the tar, into oncoming traffic.

It was over!

No one could believe what had happened to me. No one I knew had ever experienced this before. The next day, my father flew down to be with me. He was devastated and clearly wanted to console and protect me. I was so happy to see him. You need your dad in times like this, and my dad was always there.

For the next few days it was all police, greeting cards, flowers, criminal composite pictures, insurance, and no sleep. I was in my final year at university. A few weeks to go. Almost there. I couldn't afford to be derailed. I remember sitting in my room alone, making a pact with myself. 'I will ignore this ever happened. I won't let the criminals win. I'll just study hard. I'm fine! I'm moving on.' That's what I told everyone. Surely you could will the trauma away?

I managed to convince my father and my friends. In those days, no one thought of trauma debriefing. A big hug, some chocolates and a friendly ear from my family and friends seemed to do the trick. I took the entire incident, wrapped it in a neat bundle, threw it out of my life, and hit the books hard.

And the drinks harder.

I was also waiting for other news. News that could be compared to winning the career lottery. Finally, it came.

```
Telegram: 11 November 1992
11 Trelawney
Liesbeeck West Road
Rosebank
Cape Town
Dear Mr Carastavrakis
It is with great pleasure that we confirm your
   acceptance into the Lever Brothers Graduate
   Training Programme commencing in January
   1993. You will be appointed as a Marketing
   Assistant in the OMO Washing Powder brand
   office. A relocation officer will be assigned
```

```
to you to ensure all the details of your
   move are finalised soonest.
We wish you all the best for your exams and
   look forward to your move to Durban in the
   new year.
```

I'd done it! I'd got the dream job everyone in my class wanted: a marketing position in one of the biggest consumer-goods companies in the world. Interviews had been held on campus earlier that year and I'd got through the first round. Their head office was in Durban, and I'd been flown there for the final interview. It was a real honour and a very novel experience to be flown across the country, put up in a fancy hotel and have all the details looked after. I was now playing in the big league.

I really enjoyed the interviews and remember charming the panel with some interesting stories about my life. I was well informed and read a lot about current marketing topics.

I was super prepared when it came to Lever Brothers. I'd researched all their products and the marketing they had done in the past few years. I really wanted this job and knew I was up against many others from around the country. I had to get it. It was a ticket to a new city, a new adventure, a new life. It was also a certain future. No job-hunting, no borrowing money to get by. Best of all, the relocation would be paid for, along with a relocation allowance.

I had landed with my ass in the butter. My future was set! All I had to do was get through exams. Ignore the hijacking and get through the next few weeks.

I managed to graduate in the top third of my class, with better marks than I expected. I now had a Business Science degree, with Honours in Marketing. I was one of a few who had completed it

Graduation Day with Mom in 1992.

in four years and had never failed a single subject. I knew that by moving on and studying hard I could beat trauma. It had worked!

Summer holidays came; my last summer of freedom. I had an Honours degree under my belt, the best job in the world, and all the potential cash that came with it.

I felt like the King of Cape Town that summer.

Beach all day, party all night. The nights were particularly fun, with the usual clubs where all my friends were. I got drunk every night, way over the legal limit for driving.

I would leave the clubs, drunk, and tell my friends I was going home. What they didn't know was that I would drive past the few gay bars I knew of in Cape Town. I would sit outside and watch the men come and go from those clubs. Scared that someone would notice me, I would keep moving, and often drive around the block. I so badly wanted to go in. I wanted to be a part of that nightlife. Drunk enough, I used to think that I could pluck up the courage to go in, but I never did.

I'd had a boyfriend briefly at the end of my first year, but that fizzled out. Since then, I'd played a game of deflection. I was living a lie – secretly looking at and lusting after men, while showing interest in women. It was exhausting. I had a really beautiful girlfriend in final year. We were fantastic friends and social partners. But there was nothing more on offer for me, and it didn't last.

I had become a permanent liar. A liar to the people I loved. Faking it all the time was my only way to handle the risk of being exposed. That thought filled me with horror. What would happen to me? Would my parents cut me off? Would my family, sister and cousins disown me? What would my friends say – the ones I had been lying to for all these years? Could I ever recover from that?

Do I run away and tell no one? That would be irrational! What *was* a rational response for me, however, was to drink these thoughts away. So, I did that – properly, and often. I was social and active enough to be totally distracted. I studied super hard to occupy my mind. I drank and studied with such fierce determination that I would never have to confront my sexuality. But slowly it was getting harder to ignore. So, late at night, drunk, I would park outside these gay clubs.

I did meet some guys there. They would walk up to my car and start talking to me. Clearly, they were looking to pick up a guy, and knew I was cruising for the same thing. I had denied my sexuality for so long. I needed the release, I told myself, and alcohol gave me the courage to drive in search of it. Sometimes, I would hook up with a guy and go back to his place or mine.

I started a secret gay life.

I was a little drunk at times, but I convinced myself that I knew what I was doing and with whom.

These were the days of full-blown AIDS – before ARVs. You got it, you died, is what we were all told. No problem, I would keep safe. As safe as a drunk guy can stay. My long summer was becoming less a summer of freedom than one of denial, paranoia and drink. Perhaps the tropical surfing town of Durban would give me a chance of real freedom?

DURBAN DAYS

'My Costa got the best job out of all of his graduating class.'
— MOM

It was Sunday morning, 6:00, February 1994. I had been in Durban for a year already. I'd ended the long night of drinking on another beach – this time in Umhlanga, a little way north of Durban. I was in dark jeans and a sweaty white T-shirt. I reached for my Camel Lights and sat watching the sunrise, finishing my big night out, with my sunglasses on.

A man then ran past me.

He had short blonde hair and a power body, and was running in a black Speedo. Yum! He was about my age, and was running with a tyre over one shoulder. Umhlanga beach is steep in sections and has a huge camber. *Carrying a heavy tyre while running on a soft beach must take ridiculous strength*, I thought. A fantastic cross-training exercise was being performed in front of me by a beautiful vision of an athletic man. A real badass athlete!

Taking a long, deep drag of my Camel Light, I realised I was a badass as well, but of a different kind. Not the good kind.

I'd had another night of drinking and dancing at Club 330. A regular at this club, I hung out in the VIP section. Here, all the freaks and the fashionistas of Durban would congregate. In this small room above the club, the cool would collect. I knew drugs were being done around me, but I had something inside me that always said no.

I was terrified of drugs and would always dodge them. Why did I need them? I had so much fun with my alcohol and social life, I didn't need more. I was shit scared of my addictive side, which was becoming clearer to me as I got older. This kind of kept me away from drugs which was a blessing of sorts. Alcohol can keep you functioning on a high level if you have it under control.

But did I have it under control?

Still drunk, the picture of bad health, I was sitting in a beautiful natural setting that was a health and training dream. I was abusing my body, and my chances in life. I hated myself.

How had I got to this point so quickly in Durban? I was meant to flourish on my own. I was meant to shine. How could I, in the double life I had created?

One part of me had my corporate life. My brand office was the largest profit contributor to the entire group. We had the largest budget and, with it, huge responsibility. What I struggled with was fitting into a corporate mould. Keeping time was easy for me, but attention to detail, admin, office politics and keeping my mouth shut was more difficult. I would mess up all the time. I would round up budgets to the nearest R100 000 as it made things easier, and Accounts would have a heart attack about the variances I used to report monthly. You just don't do that shit!

Details bothered me, and I was in a detail-oriented position. My power came in my bright ideas and my ability to spot market opportunities. I would come alive in such meetings and added a lot of value. I was Greek and had come from a long line of entrepreneurs. Come to think of it, I didn't know many Greeks who worked for others. We are loud self-starters who don't boil our food, and we don't often work for others. *What am I doing here?* I often thought.

I had a wonderful Brazilian boss called Fabio. He was out on secondment for a few years, a placid, patient person who was great to learn from. Both coming from continental-type backgrounds, we had a lot in common. Like him, I felt like an expat in Durban. Most of the people were from white Anglo-Saxon backgrounds, different from me. Badly dressed, with little knowledge of Europe and the world outside of South Africa. Snobbishly, I just felt like many of them were not 'my people'.

Time in the company pub was hard for me. You wouldn't think so, with all the free booze. It was a small space where the women awkwardly made passes at me and men acted out in full bravado. Every Friday, I couldn't wait to leave the pub – to escape to another world I had created for myself. A world where I could be Costa. A world where I felt normal: sometimes drunk, but happy.

Hanging out in a few nightclubs and bars, I met three incredible friends, Sarah, Anthea and Paulo. The girls worked in fashion and the creative world. Paulo was also gay, and we instantly became good friends. The four of us would hang out most nights of the week and called ourselves the 'four non-blondes' after a band that was popular at the time. We would talk about life, cook, watch TV and party on weekends. They were my safe space. They accepted me as I was. Weekends were my escape time with my loving crew, tanning with surfers on the beach by day, and dressing up in the latest fashion by night, dancing to the best music and meeting new guys and crazy creatives. I had found my tribe.

I dreaded Mondays, putting on my suit and tie, going to work. Walking into the office, I would feel my chest tighten. The corporate world was choking me. Harder to hold up was the facade of being a straight man, not being allowed to talk freely about my life with colleagues I'd spend all day with.

It got harder and harder. Some weekdays I would come to work hungover. My mood was also becoming sombre at work, and a few were noticing that I had lost my spark and personality.

'Get up.' Fabio, my boss, was speaking sternly. 'What do you think you are doing?'

I looked up from the floor, where I was lying.

It was 8:30 on Friday morning. I was still drunk.

The night before had started with a bottle of black sambuca, the sticky Italian aniseed shooter. This was what I used to call 'the car bar': the bottle of booze I would drink in the car while driving to go out, or between venues, or that was available for any afterparty that would come up in the early hours of the morning after places had closed. On this night, another close friend Di and I had tickets to a Dr. Alban concert. He was a dance music showman who was massive that year, particularly with a huge hit that resonated so much with me at the time, 'It's My Life'. It was the hottest ticket in town, and my mates and I had gone big.

When the concert was over, we'd gone out hunting for more fun, and had easily found others to play with. At 4:00, the black sambuca finished, it was time to get a few hours' sleep before work.

Problem: I had lost my house keys. I passed out outside my flat in my car.

My car was already hot at 8:00 when the Durban sun woke me up. Shit! I had to get to work. No keys, nowhere to shower … no problem. I would go to work in these clothes. It was casual Friday!

'Casual', that day, would also mean white jeans full of mud around the ankles and sticky black sambuca stains. The smell of aniseed and alcohol on my clothes and breath must have been potent in the crisp, air-conditioned offices of clinical, corporate Lever Brothers.

Fabio picked up the phone and called HR. 'Hello. This is Fabio. We have a problem on my floor.' His deep Brazilian Portuguese accent sounded like he'd ordered a hit on me. He'd done the opposite, in fact. It was a very loving and caring thing, calling the HR department and admitting to them, for me, that I had a problem.

Working for a multinational sure had its perks. They had international best-practice processes to deal with people like me. A very gentle woman from HR called me up to her department. *HR people are always gentle and caring*, I thought. Just what I needed now.

She sat me down and made me a strong coffee. I could go home to rest, but before that, I would need to agree to a plan she would put into action. She said Fabio had spoken to her a few weeks before, telling her that he thought I was sinking into a depression and was moody, quiet and very unproductive as a result.

She recommended 12 company-funded, weekly therapy sessions with their appointed therapist.

'Therapy? Oh dear. A couch and a box of tissues, like in the movies? Here we go.'

But she was right. I was sleeping long hours and battling to get myself out of bed. I was also drinking way too much. I cried a lot when I was alone, and was often sad when I was not drunk or with my friends. This wasn't normal.

Yes. I needed help.

THERAPY

'For fuck sakes, make up your mind: are you gay or straight?'
— GARY, MY NEW GAY FRIEND IN DURBAN, WHEN HE
OVERHEARD ME TELLING SOMEONE I WAS STRAIGHT

Driving myself to the therapist, I knew exactly what I would open with. It was time! Before I said another word, I started: 'Hi, Allan. I'm Costa and few know I am gay. I have been hiding it all my life.'

There it was. Done. Out of the way.

Allan was a lean, bookish man. He was very softly spoken, and had a delicate and loving manner about him. I felt comfortable immediately. In our sessions, we worked through many issues. He made me realise that I presented an image of perfection to the outside world and had layers of masks that needed constant adjusting. My true essence was very different: a young man with little to prove; a gentle soul with a spiritual side. Full of hope, creative, funny, with a great sense of adventure.

But first –

Mom, Dad, I'm gay.

Sonia, I'm gay.

Extended family, I'm gay.

Friends and colleagues, I'm gay.

I owed it to my parents to share it with them first. I needed them the most, too. Some warned me against it, but how could I not tell them first? They loved me so much and deserved to know.

It was me who was hiding, and I was sure they wanted the real version of their son rather than a limited and strained version.

Of course, they were emotional. They had suspected I was gay since the lesbian runaway therapist had mentioned something about it back in 1980, but they didn't have the tools to express or handle it. Through therapy, I realised I was very much supported by my parents, and I was wrong to have thought otherwise. One thing I knew deep in my heart was that, no matter how hard it was for them to deal with, they would *never* reject me. I just knew it. My parents' love for me has always been unconditional. The few months that followed were not easy; many emotional phone calls and visits brought lots of tears.

I made a firm commitment to engage with them openly and honestly. In these months, they may have not shown support for some of my ideas, but the intention was there. Not once did I feel that I would be rejected. What more could a man ask for?

The Greek community and my extended family were easier to tell. I hadn't lived in Joburg for many years, which made it easier, but what made it easier still was that I decided to always be the one to bring it up first and talk about it openly. The community can be very toxic with its salacious gossip, and I could've been a casualty. Imagine the potential for this, arriving at a large community lunch after church one day?

'Look, it's the Carastavrakis boy. Such a sweet kid. I hear he's gay,' would follow in a whisper. 'What an awful thing for his parents.'

An easy way to avoid this was to give them nothing to talk about. There were no secrets anymore. No sordid details. Full disclosure.

You know what happens to gossiping, harmful people around people like me at a church lunch? They smile, hand you a slice of baklava from the lunch table, and move on to talking about other people.

Then, 'Costa, let's face it. You are not made for the corporate world either,' Allan said.

What a relief! I was hiding that as well, and Allan and I came up with a plan for me to look at life beyond Lever Brothers. Travel, and a new career!

Near the end of my sessions, Allan said something I found very uncomfortable. 'Costa, I think you have tendencies towards alcoholism,' he said in his slow and mellow voice.

'Alcoholism?' I responded, surprised. 'But alcoholics drink every day and have vodka for breakfast, don't they?'

'Well, no. Strictly speaking, an alcoholic is someone who abuses alcohol to a degree that it begins to look like he depends on it. It is someone who needs a drink to cope with certain things. I think you have a tendency towards binge drinking. This is something you need to watch.'

'But I just have fun, and it's only on weekends.'

'What about the regular Thursday night out with your friends that you talk about? That would make it a four-day weekend.'

'Well, we don't drink on Sundays! So, it's still a three-day weekend.'

Denial!

I was trying to worm my way out of this discussion. He had seen a serious pattern I wanted to avoid. The session ended.

'Can you believe he called me a bloody alcoholic?' I said to the three other non-blondes. 'I mean, what the hell?'

'Ridiculous!'

At that moment, a waitress came up to our table.

'Four Long Island Iced Teas, please.'

MIAMI VICE

'Find the beat.'

— MY SISTER'S FLAMENCO DANCE TEACHER

Hola, soy Constantino, y soy gay (Hi, I'm Constantino and I'm gay).

Full name. Full disclosure. Full-on.

With a Eurorail ticket, some money in my pocket and my new honest, open identity, I was free to meet whom I wanted, say what I wanted and be what I wanted. It was the most liberating feeling just to be myself. I could breathe. I could talk freely about my heart's desires to anyone I met. There was no more hiding.

In Europe, I fell in love and fell out of love, spent many days on the beach, and many nights in countless nightclubs. I drank a lot, but not too much. Money was tight, so I held back a little. Besides, I felt good. Not much alcohol needed here.

The end of my European trip was in Greece. If I thought I was comfortable and happy in the rest of Europe, it was nothing compared to how I felt in Greece. Men are very expressive there, and even a taxi driver feels nothing about talking to you with his hand on your leg when you're sitting in the passenger seat next to him. The straight men I met were happy to hang on me while talking to me about my gay life. It was liberating to be accepted and even celebrated by other men.

But my head would hit the ground hard a few weeks into my Greece trip with a smackdown from none other than the Big Man

Free in Santorini, 1994.

Smoke break in Mykonos, 1994.

upstairs, God Himself.

My mother is a religious woman whose faith is the foundation of her life. She was the spiritual guide in the family. She knew I was going through a turbulent time and thought it would be good for me to seek some spiritual counsel. I agreed that it could help, but who did she have in mind?

Like a good mother, only the best would do for her son, and like a good Greek, she had connections. Her church connections went all the way to the top. Yes, to the 'Pope'. Well actually the Archimandrite of Alexandria himself. In our church, we have five such leaders, or Pope equivalents, worldwide, and I got a private counselling session with one of them at his Athens apartment. When I heard who he was I had some reservations, but when

Mamma gets you an appointment with the Pope, you go!

His home in a fancy suburb of Athens was sparsely furnished. I expected walls dripping with icons and gold crucifixes. Not here. He was a simple and gentle man. I actually knew him from when he'd been in Johannesburg as a priest, and felt instantly comfortable with him. He offered me Greek coffee (of course) and *glyko* (syrupy-sweet candied fruit), and we sat down to talk. I was dying for a cigarette but had to hold back. Unfortunately, and uncharacteristically, he was one of the Greek Orthodox priests who *didn't* smoke, so I sat nervously playing with my fingers.

We spoke about my recent travels and then got to the last few years and troubles I was going through. I told him how I had resolved to live my life my way and come out the closet and follow my happiness. He nodded supportively and then we sat in silence as he obviously searched for the right words.

'Costa. You are welcome in the House of God. Your choice of sexuality is not.'

When I left his home, I decided not to take a taxi. I needed to breathe. I was crying, and aimlessly walking the streets.

Great. Not even God was on my side. Officially – the 'Pope' had said it to my face.

A sadness crept in at the end of my stay in Greece. I'd been getting so comfortable in my new skin as a gay man, openly being me and living life to the full. I was drinking, but not excessively, and that was probably because I felt like myself most of the time. Standing on a hot August night on the pavement of a busy street in Athens, I felt rejected and unloved. Emotional and sad.

My spirits would be further dampened by the move to London I'd been planning for some time. I arrived there from hot, holiday Greece just as the city's damp and dreary autumn was starting. I lasted 11 excruciating weeks. The darkness and hard work

*Two random hotties with me in front of Gianni Versace's house
in South Beach, Miami.*

depressed me even more. All around me I saw little grey people
following one another around.

It was time to take what little money I had, follow the sun
and go west, to Miami. It was late 1994, and a resurgent Miami
was all about Versace, Madonna and South Beach, derelict Art
Deco buildings next to remodelled delights, beautiful people,
and models and film crews everywhere. I was now one of them!
Perhaps I could find fame and fortune, here where I knew I would
be accepted. Denim shorts and rollerblades on!

Men, men and more men. I was a young man, and caught the

97

eye of many. There was fun to be had in the form of weekends away in Key West, long days on the beach, rollerblading on Ocean Drive, and hot nights in the nightclubs.

My drinking ramped up as I was in a permanent state of party. Conversations were always about sex. These were the early days of ARVs, but many were still dying of AIDS. They used to call South Beach 'heaven's waiting room'. Many would find out that they were positive, cash in their savings and policies, and come to live it up here till they died. I met many such men, and had sex with them. Always protected sex, but clearly risky when I was drunk.

I even managed to find a temp job, settle for a few months and earn some cash.

One day, I woke up and knew it was enough. I opened the local gay magazine and saw a picture of myself in denim shorts at a foam party, surrounded by hot men all covered in foam. I looked at this picture and knew I was done. Life had become way too pink. Gay parties, more parties, dinners, restaurants, clothing stores, gay events and only gay acquaintances. I did not feel like I was living a well-rounded life. I was tired of hot and hotter men. There was a fake side to it all; the mindless chatter and cruising and dating were boring.

Madonna wasn't calling me for lunch. I wasn't hot enough to be included in the troupe that hung around Versace. What the hell was I doing there?

I missed my brain. I missed a bit of my soul. I missed home. I wanted a career, and to build a life for myself. This was not going to happen so far away from my home, working illegally, with so little money and so few real friends or connections. I craved reality. I knew I was made for more.

My moral compass reset, I booked a flight home in the middle of 1995.

Another relocation. For the first time, I thought I may already be too far gone. Others my age were already in their third year of building great careers. While a side of me was high-functioning, I was still a man with big problems.

You'd think coming out of the closet would have solved my problems. It hadn't.

ENTREPRENEUR WORKAHOLIC

'Look at Peter. He is very successful. He has a Mercedes.'
— PRACTICALLY EVERY GREEK AUNTY AT CHURCH

I'm Greek. What do we do? We work for ourselves and make money. Of course, I've been sold the 'slave-to-work' model all my life. 'Nothing comes easily.' 'Only hard work pays off.' It's like it's not worth it unless there's blood dripping onto your accounting ledgers. There is no such thing as a free moussaka. Perhaps self-worth would come to me with money – and, most of all, recognition as a young Greek millionaire!

MAKING A BIG SPLASH IN THE BIG CITY
Style magazine, October 1997

There is a great deal of blah and waffle about Johannesburg's inner city at the moment. There's talk of saving it, of urban renewal, of upgrading it, of bringing it into line with other cities of the world. But Johannesburg doesn't need talk, it needs success stories. Here's one:

When Chantal Gussenhoven and Costa Carastavrakis relocated their clothing business from a plush Sandton office park to downtown Johannesburg people thought they were mad. They are however pioneers in the reclaiming of Johannesburg with nothing but sheer entrepreneurial drive. Their clothing company The Style Factory supplies

Style *magazine photo shoot*, 1997. CREDIT: PETER BAASCH.

uniforms and outfits to some of South Africa's biggest cor-
porates and 5-star hotels. Their two-year-old business is
surprisingly successful, considering the doldrums facing the
South African clothing industry.

We had arrived. My business partner and I had started out in a
backroom of her house shortly after I had returned from Miami.
We were old friends who had a long and shared history. Most of
all, we shared a very strong drive to be self-reliant and independ-
ent. We wanted to be our own boss and make it big. A dose of guts
met a pinch of madness and we started this business with a little
over R20 000 in capital each. Luckily for me, my parents allowed
me to stay at home and live off them. Yiayia was amazing, and

showed her delight at having her little boy back home by leaving stashes of petrol money in my trouser pockets. Luckily, she left a little extra too, which meant I could have a social life! What a great start to a business!

Two tough years passed – years in which, statistically, most businesses fail. We made little to no money and reinvested everything. We were young, driven and hungry for success. I had found a new meaning and purpose in work – some would call it a new addiction, perhaps. But that's a healthy addiction, right? It's right to kill yourself for the weakening rand! That's what I heard from immigrant Greek culture, and what I told myself.

I worked a lot. Long hours. Hard, stressed hours. I loved it.

Media coverage followed, and some overseas contracts started rolling in. So did the money. We made a lot of it. In our late 20s, we were self-made, and gained the respect of many people – including my family and peers, which filled my ego with importance. These were definitely the ego days, when I chased the money and what it could buy.

I was living in a new city again. Sure, it was the city I grew up in, but things were different now. I was different now. Time to make new friends and create a new life for myself. The best way to do that was to get social; I knew exactly how to do that.

Work was all-important, and I would prioritise it over drinking and partying. I had made it a hard and fast rule to not drink during the week. Sometimes this rule was bent for the odd party, but I mainly kept to it.

But come weekends, I was back to my old antics. Lots of drinking, drunk driving and dancing.

RAPED

1997. There was no internet in those days and, not having much of a gay circle of friends, the only place to meet guys was in bars or at cruising spots. One notorious spot was Zoo Lake, where guys would drive around looking for another guy to meet and maybe hook up with.

One night, after dinner at a friend, it was time to drive home. I didn't live far from Zoo Lake, and a combination of loneliness and horniness came over me, as it often did. I decided to drive around the lake and see who was there. There was certainly a thrill attached to it. There was a chance you would strike it lucky and meet another guy who was quite cute – and who knew what that could lead to? While gay sex had been decriminalised at that time, there was still danger attached to cruising. Often, guys would get busy outside their cars, which was clearly indecent exposure, and illegal. I wasn't too bothered, though, as I would stay in the relatively safe confines of my car. What could go wrong with a closed window and my foot on the pedal?

Lights flash behind me and I see familiar blue police lights, bright in my rear-view mirror. I've been slowly driving away from the lake, but the police van right up behind me flashing its lights is a clear signal to pull over.

Fuck!

I stay in my car and wait for them to approach me.

Hang on, it's only one guy. Okay, perhaps it'll be easier to convince him?

'Get out your car,' he says. 'I'm sure you've been drinking. Where is your driver's licence?'

No I haven't! Fuck. I also can't find my licence.

'Is this car even yours? What's your name?'

'Yes, it is. I promise its mine. Costa Carastavrakis.'

'Well, I will call the number plate in. We will see then.'

Over the radio in front of me, he calls in the number and we wait for the response.

'No record,' he says.

'Oh, maybe they aren't updated,' I say. 'It's a new number plate.' I wasn't lying. It was literally a month after the plates in our province changed, and I had recently got mine done. They must have had the old number on their system.

'Look up my old one, starting with NBZ.'

He turns his radio off and stares at me. This was going to go his way.

'I know what the fuck guys like you come here to do.'

'No, listen, this is really my car.'

'I'm not stupid. You faggots want to fool around here, don't you?'

'I have my licence at home. I promise I can go fetch it and bring it back.'

'Fuck you. You think you can do what you want here? You deserve to be fucking shot!'

'No really, I live close by. It's two minutes away.'

And there I made the biggest mistake of the night.

'Really? Okay, then, go fetch it and prove it to me.'

If I could prove the car was mine, he would ignore the fact that

I had no licence. Better yet, I lived in a complex of over 100 units. Nothing would happen.

I drove into my complex and parked next to my neighbour in my allocated slot. The police van followed and parked right up behind me, parking me in.

No problem, I thought, I was on home turf, neighbours all around me, I would run up the stairs and quickly fetch the ID.

I did that while he waited in his car. I ran up the single flight of stairs and fumbled for my keys. Frightened and disoriented, I didn't notice he was standing right behind me as I opened the door. I walked in and he followed. That wasn't supposed to happen. He closed and locked the door behind him.

This was bad.

'Nice place. How can a guy your age live like this?' he started. 'Daddy bought you this flat? I know brats like you. You're a brat, hey?'

'No, I work for myself. I have my own business. This is all mine.'

I was indeed lucky – my parents had paid for half of my flat. My first pad was the best landing pad any guy could ask for! But he wasn't going to get those details.

'Own business? Kak! Where?'

'It's called The Style Factory.'

'Where?'

'Selby area.'

'Oh ja? Where in Selby?'

Fuck him, I thought. I was definitely not making this up, and gave him the full, long, detailed address.

'Third Floor, Genop House, 15 Hulbert Street, New Centre.'

'Oh yes – I know it. The one downstairs from HI Merwitz Saddle Makers.'

I froze. Our business was in an obscure industrial part of town.

I had lived in Joburg my whole life and never heard of that area before, let alone that street or building. I now had a cop in my house, with a gun, who knew exactly where my business was. In that instant I thought he may have been following me for a while. How would he know where I worked? What the fuck was going on? A nightmare I couldn't ever have imagined was happening in my living room.

He must have seen the fear on my face as he took the gun off his hip and held it in one hand. He then stepped up to my face and, with his other hand, he took my hand and put it on his crotch.

About four hours later, the sun was starting to come up. I was lying in my bedroom, naked, next to him, my head snuggled under his armpit – that is where he made me put it. He was snoring, and I had not slept a wink. Must have been two hours I'd lain there, frozen. His gun was still next to him on the other side of his head.

'Try something funny and I will use it,' he said a few times that night.

I'd fantasised many times about how I would take that gun and blow his brains out. I'd seen *Pulp Fiction* a few years before, and could see his brains splattered all over my wall. I played that over and over in my head. But I did nothing. I didn't know how to handle a gun. He stirred and woke, and tried to hug me a little. I just lay there, the taste of his semen in my mouth and the smell of his day-old police-uniform sweat all around me.

'Make me a cup of coffee,' he said.

Was this a date gone wrong? What the fuck was going on? What I did know was that he'd finally let go of me and I got out of bed.

I could run out of the apartment, but I was naked. *Best I behave and let him go*. He looked relaxed. Calm and agreeable, even. He would leave – all it would take was a cup of coffee.

I put shorts on and went to the kitchen. I heard him dressing and going to the bathroom. Soon he would be gone. *Make the coffee. Quick!*

As I was stirring the coffee, I had an idea. I snorted a huge load of wet snot back through my nostrils into my mouth. I then spat that huge dollop of snot into the coffee and stirred it in. The hot water diluted it quickly. If he was going to leave, it would be with about two huge tablespoons of my snot in his coffee.

We stood in the living room while he drank the coffee and put his gun back on his belt and turned his radio on to clock back in. I watched him quickly drink that whole cup. Every last warm, snotty sip.

'I know where you live. I know where you work. If you tell any-one, I will find you. You hear me?'

He left.

For the first two days, I told no one.

Serves me right. What was I thinking, driving around drunk?

I should have fought back. I mean, he wasn't that big.

Cruising for sex is wrong. This is what happens when you play with fire.

Then, a total breakdown, and full disclosure to my family and friends.

Chantal found me a tough criminal lawyer, whom I went to see. He told me I stood no chance on the stand and that my story would look much like consent because it happened in my own home, with no visible force used against me or signs of struggle in my home or on my body. He coldly advised me to get a boy-friend and move on. What an asshole. This advice, from a guy who was gay himself.

My parents were super supportive. I moved back home for a week as I could not stand to be in the bed where I'd been choked, manhandled and forced to perform depraved acts on a smelly, ugly man. I went with my sister and her family to the coast to get away. I was surrounded by so much love – and confusion. Both theirs and mine. *How do I make sense of all this? How do they?*

All I got was constant support, love, acceptance and understanding.

I went to Lifeline for trauma counselling for 12 weeks. Trying to cope was harder than ever – I went back to work after a few days as Chantal said she wanted her business partner back. She had no clue what I was going through – I didn't have a clue myself.

Everywhere I went, he was there. When the lift opened at work, I saw his face. When I opened my door at home, he was there. I needed to cope. I needed a mask. The one I took on had a very hardened form – hardened with cement. The cement of shame. The shame of being raped.

Before the rape, I'd been trying hard to cope with my life, trying to learn self-love and self-worth. Trying to find my own way in this new world, as a gay man in a new city. This was a smackdown. Being made to feel disgusting and totally worthless, and threatened with a gun, was way beyond what I had experienced before. Way beyond whatever the bullying at school may have done. While some of the feelings were the same, this was way worse, and hit hard. At home. Violated in the intimate space of my bedroom.

After 12 weeks of counselling, and much family and friends time, things started to shift – on the surface, at least. They had to: I had to move on. A few more whiskies than usual and things felt better already. Actually, I needed a lot more booze to cope.

But I didn't want to cope. I needed to block this out entirely. I needed to wipe myself out.

I was going to need something stronger.

I always told myself I would never take drugs, but a friend of mine who lived on a farm near town would always talk about the good dagga, or weed, they used to grow near her, and how they used to smoke it for a chilled-out, good time.

I could do with some chilling out! Life was stressful, I was really wound up about work, and the rape trauma would not leave me.

'Get me a box,' I said. In those days, weed was mainly supplied in a small matchbox. I got mine and hid it for the perfect day.

Very soon, that day came. I just needed to zone out, I told myself.

No way was I going to tell anyone. I was the one who had always been against drugs. Most of my friends had tried this stuff, but I was not about to admit that I had, too. Drugs were bad, and not for me. That was the story I fed the world. Today, I needed to see what it was all about. But not socially, how other people start. I would do it alone.

I bought some Rizla papers at the grocery store and came home to make my very first spliff. How hard could it be? I took the little box and crudely rolled most of it into one single joint. It was the size of a Cheech and Chong spliff. I didn't know any better, and lit it. The loosely packed dope smoked and crack-led. I inhaled tons of smoke and, in four or five drags, most of it was finished. The taste was vile but the head buzz was something very nice and new. I was high and started feeling numb. This was a feeling I knew, but something different crept in. I was lame. Totally mute and lame. Alone in my apartment and stoned for the first time ever, I lay down on the floor in the middle of my living room. Staring up at the ceiling, I could see women coming

Rollin' and smokin'.   *Wild Greek wedding ways.*

out of the walls. They were holding tapestries and were stitching their way around while walking in my flat. Trippy stuff. Hilarious giggles started.

Then I passed out.

Waking up with the most revolting taste in my mouth, I remember thinking this wasn't for me. The loss of control and hallucinations were very uncomfortable. When I was drunk I was a bit sloppy, but it was still fun, and something I knew how to handle. I could be social when I was drunk, but didn't know how that would work when I was stoned. Best I stay away!

I'd crossed a barrier, though. I had heard that drug use was progressive and that things could get worse. By avoiding weed, I thought, that wouldn't happen to me.

HOOKED ON A MAN

'Afto to *LOVE*, afto to *LOVE!* (*This LOVE, this LOVE!*)'
— YIAYIA, REFERRING TO LOVE AS SOMETHING TO BE
CAUTIOUS OF AND SAYING IT TWICE FOR DRAMATIC EFFECT

Addiction is a cunning enemy. I was about to learn that it does not only take the form of a substance. It comes in many forms, and for me the next one was love – or what I thought was love.

Howzit, Andrea, I texted.

Hellerrrrr, she responded.

We had our own little best friends' lingo. Andrea is a gorgeous, tall woman with long, dark-brown hair. She is impeccably stylish and has a strong personality. She is super funny but, more importantly, solidly reliable and loyal to our friendship and me.

We shared a similar love of fashion and all things creative, but mostly we enjoyed hours of intellectual conversation about life and human relationships. She belonged to a group who studied Carl Jung weekly and, by association, I became an armchair Jungian. At that time I'd had a boyfriend, Ronald, for a few years, and she knew our relationship dynamic well.

What you doing? she texted.

Nothing. Ronald and I are just at the pool.

Born in what was then Rhodesia, Ronald was a successful corporate-finance man I'd met just as my Style Factory business was taking off. Together, we were very ambitious. We were both

Andrea.

in our early 30s, making good money, and aspired to living well.
Together, we bought a very large property with an old house on
it in the luxurious suburb of Houghton in Johannesburg. It came
with four garages, housekeepers' quarters, and plenty space for
the newly adopted dogs to run. This house, I believed, showed we
had arrived – as individuals and as a couple.

Are you still with him? she replied.

Now I was confused.

But you had lunch with us two days ago? I responded.

Oh, just hoping you got rid of him between now and then!

Stop it! I told you not to go there.

I knew what she was doing. She was being a brat and protective at the same time. For the past few months, she'd been putting pressure on me to see things for what they were. Over the years, Ronald and I had broken up and got back together again many times, each time more dramatically than the last. I obviously included my close friends in all the details – details that Andrea would mirror back to me, along with an analysis of what was going on.

We have discussed this before. You know I love you but I can see you're not happy. It is not working and you are a full participant in all this. Own up for your shit and move on. He is certainly to blame for some stuff, but the two of you are toxic together. Get rid of him. Find yourself and move the fuck on, she replied.

Andrea was right. I had recently realised that Ronald was a narcissist and that I would often lapse into classic empath behaviour. I would put his needs first; let him decide who we saw and when we saw them. How we would spend our money, and how much. He was moody, which would sometimes mean he would ignore me for a few days while he stewed when something had happened that had displeased him.

Sometimes, he would be in a mood for a reason; sometimes, for no reason. No matter what, I was damned if I was the reason and damned if I wasn't.

Our fights were huge: as often as I played the empath and placated and soothed the narcissist, I would also look at this picture for what it was and lash out. I would remind myself that I was successful in my own right. In fact, I was more successful than him. I was a grown man with my own life and full responsibilities. Why the hell was I taking shit from him?

Fuck it! Then, I would pick a fight. Punches never flew but coffee cups were launched across the room. After a few days, however, I would normally be the one who would concede, and we would make up. Each time I let this happen, I would let a piece of myself go and a part of me would die. My manipulation at the hands of the narcissist and our joint toxic behaviour would deepen, and I would feel worse about myself.

Since meeting him, something had developed. I was clearly hooked on him. I was hooked on the fighting and the drama. I will admit that I even helped create some of it and was a willing participant in it. I thought I was in love. I thought we had a relationship based on the right values and shared goals, like other couples had. Instead, what was happening was that both of us were playing out our own pain dramas and using the other as bait in our shared emotional dumping ground. I hated him at times. I even stopped finding him attractive, and would loathe his presence before each of our regular break-ups.

Then we would get back together again. The chemistry was back, along with all the good feelings, attractions and obsessions. The drama kept me hooked, the constant vacillation between man of my dreams and pariah of my heart.

My parents and friends could see I wasn't happy, and Andrea was certainly not the only person putting pressure on me to leave. But I had a problem: low self-esteem. I found validation in love and, increasingly, even in rejection. I held onto love when it was going well and when it wasn't. Love, and my addiction to it, were destroying me. It consumed all my thoughts, and guided all my moves in life and relationships with others. Ronald and I weren't suited, and we should never have gone past the first break-up. But the addiction was just too strong.

The drinking had subsided when we were together. My successful business and this relationship took priority. Only, the latter was a complete failure most of the time. Family and friends were pushed aside as my drug of choice became the centre of my attention and object of my affection and time. This drug sustained me for a few long years, as our pathology played out.

Close to break-up time, I would be struck by a sense of guilt. I would think, *Greeks don't divorce. We stick things out. Work it out!*

One thing that made it feel better for me was milestones. I would get hooked on these, too, and the prize they held for me: a sense of validation. *Another month together. I have a boyfriend – I must be okay. He loves me, most of the time. I'm sure he doesn't mean to ignore me for two full days. I must deserve it when he does. One year together. We have real love going on here. He is right, perhaps my family doesn't want the best for me. Another year together – we must be really close. This must be love. He must know more than I do about life. There must be a good reason for him to keep my family and friends away from me.*

Years of on and off, good and bad. Years where the highs got higher and the lows even lower.

A big fight followed by a make-up trip to France. An abusive streak ending with a cruise to the Seychelles. Walking out on him, then buying a lavish house together a month later.

Everything was lived and fought and played out to the max. My addiction was in full swing; it needed only attention and validation to keep it going. Negative or positive, it didn't matter: both love and hate could ignite it.

During one of our break-ups, he asked me to pay back the money he'd spent on a holiday that had been a gift. Vindictive and spiteful, he insisted I pay him immediately upon us breaking up that time. I didn't have the money then, and he became more verbally abusive than ever before. Frightened, I went to my father to ask him for money.

Ronald was exceptionally polite in front of my family and even came across as caring towards me. My father accepted Ronald as my partner, but my erratic behaviour over the years made him question the facade we kept up in front of family. He kept his feelings to himself and tried his best to allow me to live my life the way I wanted to.

He was horrified when I knocked on his door desperate for money and some comfort after yet another break-up. Always loving and caring towards me, he got upset seeing me hurt like this. He would obviously help me, as this was the kind of supportive father he was. That night, he wrote out a cheque for the amount I needed and handed it to me. Always a real gentleman and soft in his manner, I saw a different side to him that night: he looked at me with rage in his eyes and said, 'Get rid of him!'

One week later, I went back to Ronald. Hooked!

This time, however, it was different. A part of me seemed to be stronger than before. A little fire was burning inside me, and seemed to burn brighter than Ronald's efforts to put it out. I got a bit more opinionated than usual, and was less caring than before. Ronald was confused by this change in my behaviour. I was finally seeing some cracks in his armour and that gave me strength. He was giving in a little more than usual, and the tide was turning. The empath was evolving, leaving the bully uncertain. For these few months, our time together was very strained.

It was also the time in my life when I was doing *The Artist's Way* course, the one that got me writing poetically about my 12-year-old self. My spirit was rumbling, and the internal work I was doing was about to bring about change. I was becoming esoteric – writing and creating things all the time. My practice involved more incense-burning, bells and chimes than Greek church. This newfound spirituality was a refreshing change, moving me from looking to Yiayia's dogma for answers to yoga's downward dog.

Past life regression therapy? Bring it on! I found a wonderful, serene man named Alan who came across as trustworthy, emotionally responsible and full of empathy. Just what you needed in a man about to take your hand and guide you into the depths of your subconscious. I had gone to many sessions over a few weeks. During a final regression session, a familiar thing would always happen as I would walk down a flight of stairs and Alan would say, 'Look down and tell me what you see.'

In every bloody past life – well, most of them, anyway – I would see a frilly little skirt, or a pretty pair of shoes, or a woman's delicate toes.

'Are you a girl again?'

'Yes,' I would say, with an internal eyeroll. I was always a girl or woman. (Yes, yes. I know. This would make sense to all the bullies at school too!)

In this particular life, I was Rachel. And just like the other girls in many of the lives we explored, Rachel was controlled by a tough man. In this life she had been raped by a man who had always mistreated her. I looked at his face, and it was Ronald! My past life was talking to me. Once again, a man had controlled me. Once again, I was compromised at the hands of another. Silenced, thwarted and diminished, again.

I snapped out of the regression very easily this time. No need to meditate or ruminate on what I had seen. In *this* life, I knew exactly what I needed to do.

'You will never leave me,' Ronald said. Typical of the narcissist to think he had control over that, too.

Standing outside our home, next to our massive pool, I looked around at what we had built together over the years. I felt nothing.

'Watch me,' I said. In front of me, Rachel stood with her hand out, inviting me to follow her.

'If you walk away now, I will never take you back.'

It was towards the end of 2003, and my business partner and I had enjoyed a good seven-year innings together. I was restless in the business I had helped create and grow to a staff complement of more than 40, though. I was also fast reaching burnout. The constant travel and the stress of managing the business were taking their toll on me.

Looking back, I can admit that I was addicted to the work and the stress. Most of all, I was addicted to the pursuit of business and money. It took up so much of my time and energy that it was not healthy for me. I chain smoked, got stomach ulcers, and ground my teeth to deal with the stress. I always wanted more money and was prepared to work harder and harder to get it. Balance was always missing as I flew from one country to another securing new clients and servicing others. Success had its price: my sanity and my overall health. I never exercised and often ate terribly. I still had a very unhealthy relationship with alcohol; while the binges were less frequent, they were still ferocious in their strength.

I was done with the rag trade: the production nightmares, the staff issues, the currency exposure for export contracts, the moaning customers. I wanted out and decided to sell my share to Chantal. I needed to choose me, for a change.

I turned my back to Ronald too, and walked away towards a new future, one where I would look for love that was right for me, that was healthy and reciprocated. I chose me, and felt a huge relief leaving that day. I needed to carve a new future. I knew that the many shared years would take some time to untangle, but for the most part the addiction was over. I had left. I was free, surely?

Addiction was not going to leave me that easily. That weekend, I put down the drug of love and picked up another. The progression was about to take its most dangerous turn yet.

MY FIRST LINE OF CAT

'Afta ta *DRUGS*, afta ta *DRUGS!*
(These DRUGS, these DRUGS!)'
— ANOTHER DOUBLE WARNING FROM YIAYIA

A new freedom came over me. I was no longer in a controlling relationship, and had no more clients, business partnerships, and cash-flow and staff issues to worry about. I also had tons of cash from the sale of my house and my share in the business. It was time to celebrate this freedom. I booked myself a trip to see my sister and her family in the US, and to visit Mexico, and packed my bags.

Determined to live light and free of my past, I gave away superfluous stuff, and packed my life up into a small storage space. On one of the final weekends before I left, I went out alone, something I never had a problem doing as I always found it easy to make friends while I was downing a whisky.

'Coming for a line?' asked Steven, an acquaintance I had already shared a few drinks with in a popular gay bar.

'Of what?'

'CAT. I've got some good stuff on me,' he said.

I had heard about CAT and knew some people who had taken it. I had only ever been offered it a few times, and had categorised it with hard drugs that were to be avoided at all costs. The very words 'hard drugs' are just loaded with danger. All my life, I'd been warned about them, and was really scared of them. I always reminded myself about my addictive nature and told others who offered me drugs about it. I managed to stay away and knew that, if I tried them, there was a serious chance I would become hooked.

CAT is a stimulant, a powdered drug that is snorted. It has similar effects to cocaine. It originally comes from a leafy green plant grown mainly on the Horn of Africa, called *Catha edulis*, or khat. Khat chewing has a history as a social custom dating back thousands of years in Middle Eastern cultures.

I wasn't about to partake in an ancient cultural ritual, though – I was about to take the night into the gutter and use the street or artificial form, which was far more potent.

I'd heard that euphoria, sharpened senses and tons of energy would be the reward. Downsides? Who cared? I wasn't interested. I told myself I had lived in the world according to everyone else's rules for long enough. I had worked my ass off for years and played by the business world's rules well enough. I had always paid people on time, done the right thing for my staff, and served my clients and business partner honourably and to the best of my ability. I had endured my personal relationship with Ronald and all its drama – the fights, the manipulation and the games. I had even stopped smoking once or twice over the past few years and cut back my drinking.

About to embark on a trip with no responsibilities in my home country or in real life, I felt like a cage had opened and let me out. I'd behaved for long enough. I wanted out. I was proclaiming myself as reckless, and was fine with that. I was justified in doing so.

Or so I thought.

'Ja, sure, I'll have some,' I quickly answered Steven, and off we went to a bathroom. I'd now become one of those people who went two by two (or more) to the bathroom to use drugs. He cut a line, just like I had seen in the movies, and offered me a straw.

'Hang on, I haven't done this before,' I confessed. 'You go first!'

'Okay, you put the straw into one nostril and hold the other one closed, and then sniff one hard sniff. Like this!' He sniffed all the powder that he'd so neatly lined up.

Then I sniffed my line.

Immediate guilt! The kind that only a million Greek mothers can give you. This was not icing sugar off a *kourambiedes* tray. This was a hard drug.

'*Afta ta* drugs, *afta ta* drugs!' Yiayia would say, pointing to them on TV as a warning to us growing up. Exclaiming it twice, I suppose, made drugs even more dangerous. *That's it, then. I will do just this one line, then go home.*

I'm hooked! I texted my close friend Gordon the next day. I had partied all night on many more lines and tons of alcohol, and had crawled home at sunrise.

????? he texted back.

Trust me, I know myself!

What are you on about?

I had my first try of CAT, and I loved it! I promise you, I'm hooked.

Okay, I'm calling you.

No, don't! I'm still trashed, I responded. And I was. The phone rang.

'I promise, Gordon, I'm hooked,' I said to him. I was very concerned and needed to tell someone. Gordon was the closest friend I could confide in. He also knew me the best. By telling Gordon, I felt like my future self was taking over and staging an intervention before it all began.

'Oh, rubbish. It's CAT. It's not that hectic and you can't get hooked after one hit. You are just being paranoid. So, you tried it. Big deal. Did you have fun?'

'For sure, we had tons of fun. I mean, I just got home.' It was 8 am.

'Well, go sleep it off and I'll call you later. Calm down, you are not hooked, and you will be fine.'

I put the phone down.

Gordon wasn't listening to me. I was not joking. I called him to proclaim a huge event that had happened in my life. It was a confession and a warning sign at the same time.

A feeling had come over me that I couldn't explain. I'd just unlocked myself from my life into a newfound freedom. With my first line of CAT, something else had been released: something dangerous and scary that also filled me with ecstasy and euphoric freedom. The words that came to my mind about CAT were simple and potent: *Where have you been all my life?*

My sister and her family had moved to Austin, Texas. I would base myself there for a few months and do some travelling. I love my family a lot; I cherished this opportunity to spend time with them and get to know my niece and nephew, who were growing up away from me, better. In my three years with Ronald, I had drifted away from my family. It was time to close the gap. We had a wonderful, loving, family Christmas together, and I fell in love with Austin. While my sister lived in the suburban part of it, I managed to find many cultural, nightlife and gay options to excite me. I behaved and enjoyed myself, staying well within my limits, surrounded by the love of my family and all their friends.

I had always planned to go to Mexico, as I have a sense of adventure when I travel. I like going to places that are difficult

My niece and nephew,
Nicola and Theo, in Austin, Texas.

to pronounce, have little English and tons of new culture, and where no one I know has most likely ever been. I like to get a little lost as well. With no travel partner and free rein, I booked a flight to Mexico City and planned to travel in the general direction of south via bus.

The town of Oaxaca enchanted me with its culture and unique aesthetic. The ancient sites of Monte Albán, where the Zapotec dynasties ruled, the ruins of Palenque near San Cristóbal de las Casas with their *Tomb Raider* feel and intrigue, the golden Pacific beaches of hippy Zipolite and the Catholic churches of Puebla entranced me. I had new blood coursing through my veins. I was a citizen of the world, learning new things, meeting new cultures and even partaking in indigenous tribal culture open to very few.

A new connection was forming with myself in these few weeks of bliss. The road, for me, continued south and east towards the Caribbean, where I found myself in Belize.

There, on Caye Caulker island, I found Sam, a weed dealer. He promised me 'da good staaff', which, in his words and Caribbean accent, were 'fresh off da booaat'. He reminded me that it would be easy to find him later on: he pointed to his chest, across which his name was tattooed. This was the Caribbean, after all. *Of course it would be this easy to find and use drugs*, I thought. Yeah sure, let me try some again. I wasn't mad about the idea, but why not?

For the next few days, I dived the Great Blue Hole off the coast of Belize and took a boat to the remote island of Tobacco Caye. I woke up one morning and looked at the map. I realised I was almost in Honduras. How amazing was that? I had never even known where Honduras was on a map, and now I was on the verge of exploring it. My body, however, was tired of exploring. I wanted some downtime and decided to find a spot on the coast and chill for a week or two. I decided to head back to Mexico, to Tulum. In 2004, Tulum was only being discovered as a tourist destination. It has the most exquisite ruins directly on the beach, facing the turquoise waters of the Caribbean. Everyone who goes there must visit the ruins. Except me, of course.

I found a great hotel on the beach south of the ruins. It had a nudist beach area in front, and was just what I needed: some bareback, naked, free relaxation and fun. On my first visit to the beach, I met four lively, beautiful and spirited girls, who were about my age and from New York. Together, we spent the next week enjoying the beach and the sun.

They were all gorgeous. An Asian-American restaurateur, an Australian model, a red-headed New York nightclub owner, an

Alice, Marni and me in
Tulum, Mexico.

Shetal and me in Tulum.

Indian PR diva and a mad Greek-South African formed a troupe who celebrated each moment we were together. We also enjoyed the tequila and the weed together. Every day, we would get up and look at the ruins just a few hundred metres ahead of us and decide to go. But first, a few tequilas and a joint after breakfast. Day after day would pass; each day, we would fail to make it up there, choosing rather to giggle and cavort – sometimes naked – on the beach. The ruins could wait!

Together, we made a brazen and cocky team that, at one stage, had Los Federales walking in front of us on the beach, fully armed Mexican Feds who protected the tourists and watched out for narcotics traffickers.

Did this stop us smoking weed? Hell no! We were young, invincible and free. The girls made life feel even freer. Anything was possible, as they were living the American dream. All risk-takers, beautiful, intelligent and diverse, with a touch of madness. Everything I had craved in my life back home.

They had met me naked in more ways than one. Stripped of my clothes and my past, they accepted me for who I was. They asked detailed questions about my life to really get to know me. They offered advice and genuinely cared about some of the things

I had been through. They laughed at me and with me. It was a bond of friendship I had never felt so quickly before. Together, we formed a tribe of love, tolerance, diversity and fun. For a full week, we met other men, talked through the night, shared our dreams for the future and our pain of the past, played the fool, ate too much, drank, smoked and danced. We had some healthy arguments and even a big fight – the kind that old, good friends would have. It all felt so real, and it was such a joy for me to be with my tribe once again.

But the week passed quickly; soon, they were on their way back to New York and I was alone again. I felt empty. I realised I had denied so much of myself for so many years. Now, I had seen a glimpse of myself, and loved it. Sure, there had been moments of weed and tequila, but what I had felt was real love. Something I hadn't felt back home in years. I was so busy trying to make a business and a bad relationship work that I had lost friendships – and myself. I had seen myself again through the four girls. These were the relationships I was capable of building. This was the openness, tolerance and truth that my life was capable of, and I loved it.

But the girls were gone. There was no way I could feel this happy at home, I told myself. I dreaded going back: back to my old ways, my old existence. I feared losing this new feeling. I had to maintain this newfound love for my life and for myself. But how? I had tools that could easily take me back to this feeling. Tools that promised self-love and acceptance, and that offered an easy ride. So I went out that first night alone to find more of them.

The Cancún–Chetumal highway was built in the late 70s. The idea was to open the desolate but beautiful eastern Caribbean coast of the Yucatán Peninsula to tourists. Tourism developed very quickly around Cancún first, and moved southwards along what soon became known as the Riviera Maya. On the sea side of this highway are exceptional resorts, all four stars and upwards, from eco boutique hotels to spa retreats. Each one offers delectable restaurants and more lavish luxuries than the next. This highway cuts through the town of Tulum, where it becomes the main road. A few hundred metres away from the luxury of the resorts are ramshackle grocery stores and hostels that cater for the tourists who come to view the ruins, then move on. Tulum also exists to serve the local population with their regular small-town needs. I doubted that the local population benefited very much from tourism, other than by taking up the low-paying jobs of service and other such work. The town of Tulum was typical of this area: newly developed with rough, square, concrete buildings, and not much civic pride or beauty to speak of. It was a newish but already decaying town that was there purely to serve the surrounding tourist area.

I went walking that night, looking for a bar to enjoy some drinks. I saw the usual backpacker hostel types hanging around. I could have been on the Khao San Road in Bangkok. There were cheap bus deals and even cheaper excursions on offer everywhere. Some loud but good dance music thumped from a café on the corner, filled with blue light. There was practically no one in the café, but I wasn't looking for a crowd and decided to go in. I found a white leather couch, sat down and ordered some drinks. An hour or two passed. Many drinks down, I was relaxed and in my own little world. When 1:00 came, the DJ stopped playing without any notice. It seemed the bar was closing and I had to leave. I was not ready to go home. I wanted some more music and fun, so I approached the DJ box to ask him where I could find it.

'*Hola. Pardona me. Donde esta una club ahora, esta abierto?*'
My rough Spanish could at least ask where another club was
open.

'Just wait outside. I'm packing up and will be outside in a
moment,' he said with a heavy accent, but in perfect English, a
large grin on his face.

He was an attractive, lean and rough-looking guy in a simple
T-shirt and jeans. With dry, long, brown hair in a messy ponytail,
he looked like any other cool DJ. He had a very friendly face –
one I could easily trust, I imagined.

'Hi, I'm Pedro,' the good-looking DJ said when he came outside and held out his hand.

'*Mucho gusto,*' I replied.

'Got a smoke?' he asked.

'Sure.' I gave him one. 'What goes on in Tulum on a Tuesday
night after 1:00?' I asked jokingly. Since I'd stepped outside, I
hadn't even seen a car. The town had died.

He laughed and admitted that he was not ready to end the
night either. 'Wanna go smoke some *piedra*?' he asked.

I had no idea what that was, but agreed. He looked like a safe
and tame enough guy to go along with. Anyway, this was a holiday town. I was hardly in the gang-riddled slums of Mexico City.
He was also cute. *Who knows what fun could be had?* I thought.

Walking and talking, I learnt he was a freelance DJ who played
cafés and clubs on the Yucatán Peninsula. He was 28 and mentioned he had a girlfriend, which changed the outcome of the
evening for me. I was okay with that, as he was leading me to
an adventure I had no idea about. I'd never even heard of *piedra*
before. It was probably some kind of local weed. Why not try
something new?

We stopped a few blocks away, outside a very dirty, small

concrete block of a house. It had a dim light over the front door, which opened directly onto the street.

'Got any cash?' he asked. 'I need $20 for it.'

'Sure.' I handed the money over. I didn't mind; as a small-time DJ, he probably had little. Besides, he was scoring for us, so I felt the exchange was fair. He told me to wait outside, which I did. A few minutes later, out he came with a huge grin on his face, a naughty boy smile you would give a friend when you were both going to get away with murder.

'*Vamos*. I have a place we can use.' We walked further away from the town and the lights for another 10 minutes on a dark road to a derelict building.

'It's my uncle's old house. No one lives here,' he said as he opened the large front window and climbed in. 'Jump through.'

One small light went on and we were in a dusty, single-room house with a toilet and a kitchen. There was dust everywhere, dirt on the light-blue walls, and broken windows. No one had lived here for a few years, it seemed.

'I come here all the time. Chill, take a seat on the floor.'

We both sat cross-legged on the cold concrete floor. He pulled out a Coke can, a lighter, some foil and a plastic bag. He held the bag up to me and I saw it contained a few white rock-like pieces.

'They have the best *piedra*, those guys,' he said, widening his eyes.

Okay, hang on. Little white rocks. I had seen them before in movies …

'Oh, you mean crack,' I said, very calmly, trying not to act surprised. 'Cool.'

I was drunk and a little slow. I was also ready to smoke something – I just didn't know what. I also didn't really care. Going out tonight, I'd been lonely. The girls had gone and left a huge hole. That revolting Sunday night feeling before school started!

So, it was crack. Who cares? I had done CAT and come out fine. Who cared if I did crack just once? My summer of love and expression was in full bloom. This was just another iteration of events that had come into play. Besides weed, I had done nothing else in the past few months anyway.

I watched him excitedly as he prepared the Coke can, punching a hole towards the base of it and gently placing one rock on the foil at the top of it.

'Here, you go first,' he offered.

'Oh, no, you get it going first.' There was no way I was going first. I didn't have a clue what to do and was not about to admit it. I watched him balance the rock on the can and light the top and take a long and deep drag of a very fine white smoke. Unlike cigarette smoke, this did not smell of anything, really, and was very light. In seconds, the smoke had all vanished. Pedro held his deep drag in for a while, then gently let it out.

It was my turn. I managed to copy exactly what he had done, and took a very large breath. I had no burning or fiery feeling, like I thought I would. Strangely – thankfully – the smoke didn't feel like anything. I held my long breath too, slowly let the smoke out, and waited.

I wondered how long it would take. Seconds later, a rush of warmth enveloped me. My neck felt soft and my head tilted back. A huge smile came to my face. It was sheer relaxation and joy. I took a huge breath, and exhaled. This was different from weed, which only chilled you out. It was different from CAT, which gave you energy and euphoria. This felt more soothing and calming: a warm and loving feeling, almost. I felt at peace with where I was and what I was doing. Everything was going to be okay. That's what it felt like.

I lit a cigarette and enjoyed it while I watched Pedro light up another hit of *piedra* and offer it to me.

'I'm fine,' I said, still floating and enjoying myself, alone in my own little world for 10 minutes. Then it stopped, without warning or dissipating. The feeling just left me instantly and I was in a room, drunk, with a guy I didn't know and a chilled foggy vibe in my head.

'Sure, let me have some more,' I said. In one breath I was back to that place of joy and I could see he was, too. We enjoyed a few more hits, and then the rock was finished. About 30 minutes had passed and I was really enjoying myself. We lay on the floor looking at the ceiling, talking a little but not much – two men alone with their drugs, in their world of escape.

'Have you got more money?' he asked me. It was clear that, if we were going to get more drugs, I was going to have to pay for them.

'Sure. You want to get some more? Here you go.' I handed over another $20.

'Wait here. I will go get.'

I was alone in a deserted house on the dark edge of a small Mexican town, waiting for my next hit of crack to be delivered. Was this really happening? Yes, and I was in control of it, is what I told myself. I was just letting myself go this time and experiencing something new. You should try everything once, I'd heard. Live a life of no regrets, I repeated to myself. This fortune cookie psychobabble was now part of my narrative, it seemed. Perhaps it didn't extend to trying crack – but I didn't care.

Pedro returned 15 minutes later, and I was ready for more. The alcohol was beginning to wear off, and the crack too. We repeated the ritual of preparing the rock, him going first and me next. This time, I had as much as him. I wanted the same feeling, and besides, I was paying for it. He clearly had a lot more experience than me with these things, but that didn't mean he could use more than me. I got a little selfish and definitely didn't want less than my half. I wanted the most out of this crack. The hunger inside me demanded that of me and this experience. Another half an hour went by and we finished our second lot. I was now flying. This was cool; I was in another world. It felt like there were no responsibilities or dangers. Life was free.

Then he asked if I wanted more. I had more money on me and, even though I was still very high, I didn't want to spoil the mood. My first ever experience of more than one line was now a finished second bag of crack cocaine. Perhaps this wasn't such a good idea ...

'Sure.' I sent him back again. And again. Four rounds of crack! How much *was* that, exactly? Perhaps they were half portions? Perhaps it was low-grade stuff? Something big had happened. A ferocious appetite for more had been unleashed; clearly this was hard to stop. But the money had run out, and the sky was changing colour outside.

While still very high at the end of the last hit, I noticed Pedro on all fours in the room. We had not spoken much, other than to share in the ritual and conversation. We'd mostly just sat cross-legged on the concrete floor. I now saw him looking for something on the ground.

'What you looking for?' I asked, very curious. He didn't respond – he just crawled around with wide eyes. Then, he spotted a small white speck on the floor. He moistened his finger, then lowered it to the speck to touch it. It stuck to his finger. He then placed this little white speck on the foil part of the pipe. He wasn't looking for diamond chips; with the delicate precision of a surgeon, he was picking up bits of crack that had obviously fallen onto the floor during the night. He was trying to round up as much as he could for one last hit. I looked at how serious his face was, and it startled me.

Was this what crackheads did once the money had run out and the drugs had finished? Was this how desperate it got? I became filled with fear – for myself and what I would feel like after this high. I watched him have one more hit and not offer me any. There was not enough for two and his sharing mood was over.

Once he'd finished that hit, he stood up quickly.

'I gotta go. Thanks. It was nice to meet you.'

That was sudden. Was he just going to leave me here, in his uncle's derelict house? I guess we weren't exactly friends and didn't need to look out for each other.

'Oh, okay. I'll follow you out. What's the rush, man?'

He then said something to me that gave me the shivers. Something that showed me exactly the chaos I had just stepped into: the heartless world of drugs and the damage they can wreak in people's lives. 'My girlfriend had our first baby a week ago and she will be looking for me.' He left through the window we'd used to come in, and I never saw him again.

I walked down the Chetumal highway, the same way I'd come. The sun was coming up and I was in a haze. To the left, the turquoise Caribbean, and to the right, the low, lush vegetation of the Yucatán. Here, in this natural and beautiful setting of ancient Mayan splendour, I was still semi-high, and also starting to get agitated.

What the fuck? His girlfriend has a baby, and he spends the night with me, a random stranger, using crack? What kind of father does that? I thought.

I decided that sleep would be the best, and headed back to my resort. The cars that rushed past me startled me and I got even more agitated. Why did they have to speed so much? And why was the sun so bright? Shit, it was already hot! After about 25 minutes I got to my resort. The guy at the door recognised me and said hi. I was very self-conscious; I bowed my head and just walked past him. I wasn't in the mood for pleasantries. I wanted a joint to calm my nerves and knock myself out to sleep.

I reached my bungalow door and couldn't find my keys. My pockets were empty. Where the hell had I left them? How the hell could I have been so stupid? I was furious with myself. Now what? There was no way I was going to reception in this trashed state. Besides, I was tired. It all became just too much. I looked around – there was no one near my bungalow. The door didn't look very strong. I lifted one leg and kicked the door hard. Damn door wouldn't open. I kicked it again, even harder. Third kick, and the door flung open. With a fierce temper, I walked in and went straight to my bag for some weed. I needed to dull the edge. I was coming down. It felt horrible. I was hostile, and needed to zone out or I would do more damage. I smoked two huge joints and gratefully passed out. My crack cocaine bender was finally over. What had started out with a pink, cloudy feeling ended with destruction of the door that stood between another fix and me.

When I woke up I was horrified by what I had done. I was still highly agitated, but not as much as before. I imagined how people could kill for a hit, if it got bad enough. I had a new fear of that specific drug. I vowed that I was done with hard drugs; that I would never try another one again. I was overstepping the mark. It would not end well.

Lesson learnt.

Two days later, it was 2:00 and I was standing outside a club in Playa del Carmen. It is a slightly bigger town a few kilometres north of Tulum – built for tourists, with hotels, restaurants and even its own gay club. I'd been drinking and dancing and feeling the happy vibe of a fun gay crowd. A few guys inside the club said they had taken Ecstasy, and that it felt great. I was dancing and having fun, but they were on another level. Damn it! I wanted that same level.

To hell with it. I was going to get some. I easily managed to find a guy outside who was selling it. He offered me two. Why not? *One for now and another for tomorrow*, I told myself. I still had two more days in Mexico. An hour later, both of them were in my system! I was dancing with and loving the whole crowd in the club. At about 3:30 the club closed. Walking out, I bumped into the same dealers. I was already two Es down – why not try some more drugs? I'd realised there was no way I would try more crack; what else was there?

Out of nowhere, the idea of cocaine popped into my head. Yes, an expensive and classy version of crack. More my kinda thing. *Let's keep it classy*, I thought. And, of course, naughty.

'*Hola*. Do you have any coke?' I asked the dealer.

'Of course.'

I gave him the money and in seconds I was holding my first gram of cocaine. I had found it and bought it all by myself. I was beaming with excitement and pride. *Time to take this high even higher, but to do it safely* – so I decided to go back to my hotel.

Alone in my hotel room, I was really feeling trashed and high. *What would mixing all this do?* I thought. *Does high get higher? Well, let's find out.*

I had only one problem. I didn't know how to prepare cocaine and make a line. Someone else had made the only line I had ever tried for me. I was sure I could work it out, though. I remembered seeing it in a movie once. *Pulp Fiction*, I thought. Yes, Uma Thurman had some coke and did a line. I remember that. Kind of.

I tipped all the coke out onto the bedside table in my hotel room and took out my credit card. That's what Uma used, right? I made one long, fat line – about 10 cm long – using the entire packet. That's what a line of coke looked like, I thought. A bit thick, but I was sure this was how it was done. I rolled up a 10-peso note and put my nose to the one end of the line and started sniffing. About halfway through, I had to stop. My nose and throat filled with white dust and I started coughing. A bit of coke blew off the table onto the floor. A few seconds passed. I wanted to get it over with; I sniffed what was left of the line and took a deep breath in. Globs of cocaine stuck in my nose and throat.

I lay down on my bed for a few minutes and started feeling my entire face and head go numb. I didn't realise that a gram of cocaine, if done like a regular person, could be cut into at least 10 small lines. This was also Mexico's finest cocaine. Being just a hop away from Colombia must have made it some of the best you could get. Here I was, a first timer, taking almost a full gram in one go. The rest of the night was a blur: I walked up and down the town, smoking and talking to other revellers on their own high, contemplating getting another gram. Which I did, just before the sun came up.

This time, I thought to be more careful and spent the rest of the day doing one or two lines an hour. I loved the buzz. It excited me and made me feel super strong. I had tons of energy, and brilliant ideas came up all the time. There was no need for sleep, either. Most of all, I would talk up a storm, and enjoyed my points of view the most. I found myself talking to waiters, cleaners and even the guy at reception. I simply couldn't stop babbling.

The next evening, I was tired enough to crash. Besides, I was leaving the day after that, going back to Austin to my sister and her family.

The holiday of my dreams had ended with a huge drug binge. Bigger than I could have imagined: cocaine, Ecstasy and crack cocaine. I felt a certain junkie pride come over me. I felt like a badass for having done all those hard drugs. It gave me a bit of twisted urban credibility, I thought: I was someone who wasn't afraid of doing it, and I'd got away with it. But the drugs were not what I saw in my future. Experience over, I was off to my loving family for some quality downtime, before heading for New York and then back home to South Africa.

'Want a bump?' Josh asked. I'd heard that term before and understood it to mean a hit or line of something. I was right.

Within a few minutes, we were locked in the bathroom together. Right up against each other. I realised there was no cistern or ledge to cut a line on, and I asked him where he thought we would use.

He looked at me, then took a gram out of his pocket. Using the lid of a pen, he took some of the white powder, pulled it towards his nose and sniffed it.

'Here, let me give you some.' He took a little bump and put it in front of my nose. I noticed it looked less powdery than the stuff I'd had in Mexico. It sparkled, almost like crushed glass. That was odd. It definitely didn't look like cocaine. What the hell was it? What was I about to do?

I did what a person who recklessly loves drugs would do. I first took it deep into my nostril and rubbed my nose. Only then did I ask, 'What was that?'

'Tina!' he said quickly, then opened the door and took me back to the dancefloor.

This shit burned as it went in. Those little shards of glass stung while I was dancing, but soon settled. Within an hour, we were back in the bathroom about to experience more of this Tina stuff.

New York, New York.

'Is this crystal meth?' I asked him.

'Duh!' he said, offering me another bump.

I took it.

Crystal meth made me feel more than loved, more than numb. It created a whole new reality. On it, I felt like I was living a totally different life. A life that I had no control over, but whose details had all been worked out for me. All I had to do was sit or stand there and enjoy the ride: crystal meth turned autopilot on. I was not myself at all. I was living, flying, enjoying it and doing what it told me to do. I was no longer in command, and it didn't matter at all. Crystal meth promised me a smooth and delicious ride. Minutes of bliss felt like hours. I now lived in another dimension.

The meth made me feel that it was fine to give up control … *the crystal meth's got this!*

Hours later, it was broad daylight and I was on 42nd Street in New York City, surrounded by hundreds of people. People were looking at me as if there was something wrong with me. They were right.

I was trashed, alone, high, and had been standing on a random sidewalk in New York for more than 30 minutes, staring at the buildings. I knew I had to get back to the hotel and sleep it off.

This wasn't safe.

Standing at JFK, about to leave America, I recalled my beautiful family time in Austin. Being around the love and generosity of my sister and her family had been amazing. My passion for travel had been re-ignited in Mexico, with its cultural and magical discoveries. My faith in people, friends and relationships had been restored by meeting the wonderful girls from New York.

I was a little far gone on the experimental drug stuff, though. Crack, cocaine and crystal meth were the hardest of the hard drugs, heroin aside, and I had used them all. I tried to rationalise my using.

I'm just letting off steam, cutting loose a bit, I thought. I'd always have a big night out in Joburg when I was a bit stressed. This was the same. I'd contained it to the holiday, I told myself. Looking out at my plane, about to board, I decided to leave the drug stories and memories behind. I was done with hard drugs. Again. South Africa would be a new adventure. A new boyfriend, business and life. A clean life, full of possibility. I had time and money on my side. I would clean up my act.

It would be two more years before I'd be able to do that.

HEADING FOR ROCK BOTTOM

'Pou pas tetia hora? *(Where are you going at this hour?)'*,
a common whine from Greek parents who find it difficult to
understand why anyone needs to leave the house after dinner.
— MOM

B ack in Joburg, it took only a few days before I was out in a
bar looking for drugs. Some people told me to go to Hillbrow
and buy there. Hillbrow? The chaotic, inner-city-slum centre of
town? Hell no! I wasn't a junkie. I needed an upper-class version
of a drug dealer. A barman gave me the details of a friendly gay
guy, who lived in a pristine apartment in a Tuscan-styled complex
in Douglasdale – a type of Pleasantville, full of young families
and schools and good, solid, hard-working South Africans. I got
cocaine from him a few times, but realised something was wrong.
This was nothing like the stuff I'd had in Mexico. I was being
peddled crap. I called him and took it up with him. I was a consumer and I had the right to complain, I thought. I had tried and
loved the world's finest, and now I was being sold shit.

The line went dead.

I then did what any disgruntled consumer does: I took my
business elsewhere!

I hated the fact that I was using drugs in my hometown. Only
scum used drugs! I didn't want anyone to know what I was doing
– certainly not the underbelly of society I was buying from. To
maintain my anonymity, I always used a false name. I was always

Nick ('Neek', as my one Nigerian dealer would say in his heavy accent). What a joke, trying to act like someone else. I mean, they had my number. And did they really care who I was, as long as I paid? I always paid. I still had money from selling my share of the clothing business and the house I'd had with Ronald. Flush with cash, I didn't have a care in the world – but I did need to find an alternative to this crap they called cocaine in South Africa.

Within a few days, I found a dealer who sold good CAT. At the time, I found myself in an easy marketing job that had flexi hours. It allowed me to use and play as I wanted. Besides, I had money and didn't really need a job.

My using was limited to weekends, which would start on a Thursday. On one such Thursday, I would have the close shave that is common to all addicts. I was almost bust by the cops!

I'd been followed out of my dealer's place in the suburbs by the police. Their blue lights flashing, they clearly wanted me to pull over. Shit! I quickly took the CAT I had just bought and put it between my ass cheeks. They wouldn't search there. They got me out the car and asked me where I had been. I lied, of course. They searched my body and car. They said they knew where I had been and asked for a bribe. I didn't admit guilt, but offered them the R700 I had in my wallet. What kind of drug user leaves their dealer with cash on them? I was flush, after all. I'd also never buy too much at a time. I'd started using more and more; this, I thought, was my way of controlling it. Stupid. The cops took the R700 and let me go. I got back into my car and drove off. My brazen will went into full rebel mode: with their lights still in my rear-view mirror, I took my gram out of my underwear and had a quick bump while steering with my knees to free up my hands. Fuck them! Drugs made me fearless.

Once, my dealer told me he was being watched, and that it

wasn't safe for me to visit. He offered to deliver to my house: Uber Eats, before the advent of Uber! What a pleasure. But when he arrived, he had no drugs. Empty handed, he was of no use to me. Dangerously, though, he told me he'd been followed, and that he'd had to 'swallow' the bundle he'd had on him. He said he always transported it in a secure, super-tight bag that he kept in his mouth, ready to swallow it should he be caught. On the way to my house, he'd been pulled over. I dangerously ordered my dealer, who'd clearly had the cops on his tail, to go back and get me my stash. He diligently did – he needed the cash, for sure – and came back to my house. Had the cops followed him back? What did I care? I wanted drugs. He handed me a tightly rolled, black plastic bundle, full of saliva. Had this passed through his bowels before? Or through the bowels of a desperate drug mule, on its way from São Paulo to Joburg? It didn't matter; it was now being wiped of his spit and opened to reveal the dry white powder I'd been hanging on for. It was about to go up my nose …

Using wildly one night in my flat, a moment of clarity came over me. My family, my parents, my niece and nephew – what would they all think? Good Greek boys didn't use drugs. I saw them all around me, in family photos on the wall and fridge. I mentioned this to my boyfriend at the time, who occasionally used with me. Guilt swept over me. But with a drug-confused mind and a sense of humour, I had the best solution. Give up? No! Rather take down all the pictures in my home and hide them.

Guilt visited me once again when I'd bought drugs in an area near the Greek church. Perhaps I could see someone about this problem? Maybe a priest could talk to me and try to help. I called someone to get the number of the priest from that church. I called the priest, and told him I was around the corner. He invited me over.

I arrived with the drugs in my pocket and told him I had a problem I wanted to talk to him about. He was very receptive and kind. He invited me into his house full of the icons and scents of the church. We chatted about my family and general stuff over coffee and some *koulouria*, a type of shortbread biscuit. *What a good boy I am, sitting and talking to a priest*, I thought. Redemption after all. Yiayia, who had died five years earlier, would be okay with this, for sure. Perhaps she was looking down on me and a miracle would occur – the drug addiction would be washed away. Maybe the priest could help me? The gayness? Well, I didn't want that gone. First, however, I went to the bathroom. There, I took out my gram of CAT and did a line. Thankfully there were no icons of guilt in the toilet. All I stared at while rubbing my nose clean were ceramic wall hangings of white Santorini homes. I came out, finished my coffee and cut our talk short. I had some drugs to finish. Amen!

Dealers came and dealers went, and I always knew how to find them. This was before the hyperconnected world we live in now – you had to hunt them down, and I was the guy who found them the fastest. Friends and I would walk into a bar or club and, before they'd have ordered their first drink, I'd have found him, paid him, and got the first stash of the night. Junkie pride at the speed!

At one club, there was a Greek girl who was a dealer. Flamboyant, with jet-black hair and way too much makeup, she dressed like a punk version of Frida Kahlo. She loved me, and we always spoke in Greek. This pissed many people off, as she would always let me jump the queue in the bathroom.

'*Yiasou Xriso mou* (Hi, my "golden"),' I'd say, in full Casanova schmooze mode – a Greek guy seducing his Greek dealer.

'*Yiasou moro mou* (Hi, my baby),' she would say.

Her kafee was open! She was in full retail mode, and her goods were delicious!

One night at the club, it was getting late and I had used up all my drugs. I decided to look for her and found her in the toilets, rummaging through her notorious big black handbag full of drug treasure. I went up to her and she snarled at me.

'Fuck off – it's over,' she said.

'Over?'

'Yes, I've cashed up.'

'Cashed up?' Clearly this was a word she'd heard behind the *banko* in the family business growing up.

I was angry. I wanted more! 'Oh come on, you're not a corner fucking café. Give me my gram.' I mean, who cashes up their stash?

Well, she had already 'cashed up' indeed. Clearly, she had a dealer she needed to report to. Good Greek girl dealer was being diligent, and bad Greek boy Costa was sent on his way.

I hid my using from most people, although my parents had cottoned on to my drinking. They would often comment that I drank a little too much on occasion. But then again, they only saw me drinking at big weddings, and I could hold my alcohol. What made things acceptable was that I would be tons of fun and dance all the time. Every Greek dance had me at the centre of it. At weddings, I could easily finish an entire bottle of Johnnie Walker Black on my own, but nobody would know because there'd be one at every table – when yours was finished, you could move to the next table's bottle. Or, like I did at one wedding with an open bar, proceed to order Johnnie Walker Blue shooters for everyone.

The drug use was also easy to hide. In the 18 months for which I regularly used hard drugs, I made sure I didn't use during the week. I would only use when I wouldn't be seeing my parents or conservative friends or family. I don't think they ever saw me fucked – or they very seldom did. I made sure I would see my parents for dinner on a Thursday night, and then go and use for the weekend.

Alcohol was great, and I loved it. It made me the life and soul of the party. Cocaine took away many inhibitions. CAT made life exciting. Yes, it gave me energy – who doesn't want that? You feel lean and handsome on CAT. I'll take that. You also feel super sexy. That will do, too. But I wanted more from my drugs. *Perhaps I should try some hallucinogenics, like LSD and mushrooms?* I thought. Nah, I wouldn't like that. I didn't want to elaborate on existence – see things that weren't there, even if they were pretty pink unicorns.

I didn't like Ecstasy – all these strange people wanting to be my friend and touch and hug me while dancing. Fuck off! Even if, for some or other 'spiritual' reason, they could 'see' my pain, I wanted no one to comfort me. Sex was comforting – but what was the use without real intimacy?

The drugs made me exceptionally horny. My mind would wander into fantasy relationships where the very core of me was being loved and filled up by another man. Yes, I still believed another man could do that for me. I lived in a fantasy world, where I wanted it to end in an orgasmic climax – in the form of a blackout from drugs and alcohol.

This is what I'd been chasing since the first time I'd drank at age 12: a feeling of losing time, an all-encompassing numbness. I wanted to lose hours. Days, in fact. To feel nothing.

I'd been out the closet 10 years. I'd made a success of myself in business. I had a loving family and tons of friends. I'd even found a wonderful boyfriend who everyone loved, for a change:

Dana and I in Thailand, 2005.

a fun-loving Afrikaans guy named Dana, who supported me and was kind-hearted. Someone who let me be my creative, effervescent self. Everything was going right. But inside, I was full of unresolved pain and torment. I attributed my successes thus far in life to my good upbringing, and the opportunities and exposure I'd been given. A strong force of family love, close friends and a lucky, blessed life. But I didn't feel lucky. I couldn't look at myself in the mirror. I hated who I was becoming. All I saw was a liar, a cheat and a fraud. I couldn't take the pain. It was just too much.

I could have asked for help. It was all around me. I refused. I used.

A few patterns started emerging that were a clear indication that I was heading for rock bottom.

When I first started using drugs, I would use when I was out and about. Drugs were social, often shared in bathrooms with friends — or even strangers. After a few weekends of this, I got tired of everyone using my stash. I even got to the point of hiding some in a secret pocket or in my shoe. I made sure I always had my extras that no one saw or used. It started costing me more, too, so something had to change. The best idea was to move to using alone. At home. There, I could use when I wanted, how I wanted and as much as I wanted. I could also plan better and spread out my usage on a bender night. Or so I thought.

I even tried to stop all hard drugs, thinking that using only alcohol would solve the problem. So, instead of drugs, I would drink heavily. I would land up on the couch, passed out after a heavy night. Luckily, I would pass out in a safe space. But I was soon to have my first non-drug-related public blackout. I went to a club with my boyfriend, filled myself with shooters and danced the night away. The next morning, when I woke up at home, I didn't know how I'd got there. Thankfully, my boyfriend had driven us home and got me into bed. I also learnt from him that he'd had to drag me off the dancefloor, away from a stranger I'd been kissing in full view of friends of ours, who'd alerted him. Out and about, in public, among friends, I had a few alcohol blackouts over two weeks. Something dangerous was up. I decided to move back to using drugs – a way to manage the blackouts, I reasoned with myself.

Over one long weekend, Dana went away on the Wednesday night for four days. My immediate thought was to use the whole weekend. What fun – a four-day binge! I needed to plan properly, so I decided to buy the drugs for the whole duration upfront and use them steadily over the weekend. I mixed up the drug order a little – a little bit of CAT for a fast high, some cocaine to spice it up, a few joints to bring it down, and a bottle of whisky, and I started my four-day binge, alone at home.

By 10:00 on Thursday morning, all the hard drugs were finished. I'd used up the entire weekend's stash.

Fuck!

Did I stop? Hell no – I had three more days of using. So I called and doubled up the order and used for four nights and four days, with little to eat and not a wink of sleep. All on my own. All at home.

One morning, my domestic worker came in early to work. She nudged me gently to wake me up. She had let herself in, and found me on the couch. In my underwear. Surrounded by drugs and paraphernalia. My wonderful domestic worker, for whom I had great respect, had seen me in this state.

Ever since New York, I'd been looking for the kind of crystal meth I'd had there. Typical for an addict to chase that first high. I did know, however, that at that stage you simply couldn't find that kind of meth – this was evident in the very low pricing of some of the meth I'd found. I was determined to find a dealer who sold the real stuff – and I did. The good R700-a-gram stuff. That feeling of numbness, that high of all highs, was now mine. Bliss. Better yet, he would deliver to my door. My poison was now available any time I wanted it, on my doorstep.

It was the beginning of the end.

Staying in Cape Town with a friend who wasn't a drug user like I was, I went out using and came home early the next morning. I woke up to find him gone, then used some more. He came home and found me on his couch, drugs all around me – with a cigarette burnt into the wooden coffee table his late mother had left him. He had walked in on this scene with two girls behind him. He'd quickly turned and walked them out, and they'd left for the day.

In the week before I stopped using, I started seeing things that weren't there. My mind started playing tricks with me. One night, out with friends for dinner, I excused myself to go and greet a table I recognised. Going up to them, I started saying hi, and was met with a bunch of confused faces. They had never met me in their lives. They all looked totally familiar – I didn't know their names, but all their faces felt very familiar. Like I had worked with them once. I definitely knew them! I was sober, and hadn't used for three days. What was going on in my mind?

MY LAST NIGHT OF USING

'Stamata! *(Stop!)*'
— MOM

It's a Sunday night. My mouth has the metallic taste that comes with permanent thirst: stale, with a dry yet sticky feel on my tongue. My face and neck muscles are tired and stiff from endlessly contracting and contorting my features.

That's what my face does on crystal meth.

My eyes open extra wide, my jaw wider. Then I pull a huge smile to stretch my face. That's stage one. Then I use my face muscles to pinch my face at the mouth and nose.

Stretch.

Pull.

Hold the ridiculous face.

Relax.

Repeat.

Repeat.

Repeat.

Endlessly.

Hang on. This is just like the tics I had as a kid. The alcohol took them away when I was 12 but they are now back. Strange – seems the substances aren't enough to hide the nervous tension I've had inside me since I was a kid.

I pull a long, deep breath and, for a moment, I can feel my heartbeat.

Then I am in freefall.

That's what it feels like.

I've been pushed off a building and I can't stop falling.

Hang on … now it feels like I'm floating. Not falling any more.

My eyes droop and my jaw relaxes.

I'm hit by a wave of warmth and my shoulders drop.

I tense up and frown a stern face. Then the cycle starts again – contracting, contorting my features.

Then I'm falling again.

Or is this the first time?

It's a balmy night and I am alone, standing in my kitchen, leaning against the black granite counter. It's in a luxurious new apartment on the ground floor of a secure gated complex, in a posh suburb in northern Johannesburg. It's on a small, isolated hill, with a rare 180-degree view of the whole city skyline. It's a two-bedroom, two-bathroom apartment with impeccable finishes: modern slate floors, a huge wraparound wooden deck leading to the apartment's own small garden. The kitchen is modern and open plan, and I've furnished the entire apartment in slick city style with modern art on the walls and stylish furniture.

I remember the night the estate agent handed me the keys and I walked in. All the lights were off, and the city lights twinkled outside: the vast skyline of Johannesburg, with all three of its beacons – the Sandton City Office Tower, the Hillbrow Tower and the Brixton Tower – spread out before me, where I stood on my deck.

I am a king who finally has his castle, is what I thought. I'd got out of a toxic relationship, found new love, and had lots of cash in the bank and new business opportunities all around me. I was 35, lean and handsome, with a huge social circle. I lived in a city where I was very well connected. This was my hometown, where I'd gone to school and cut my teeth in business: already, I had one big success under my belt.

Clothing, money, travel, all the good things a privileged Johannesburg life had to offer: this was the life I now fully owned.

My eyes fall on my last plastic bag of meth on the granite counter. Some of the little sugar-like crystals have spilled out, leaving a dusty residue on the shiny black granite. Half the bag is left. Where has the other half gone?

My face is caught in its endless rhythm and my muscles are aching from it. But I can't stop.

I can smell something bad. Time slows down as I look around to find the source. It is my armpits. They smell wrong. Not the smell from a hard workout – salty and manly. No, it's a rank sourdough smell. Is it only my armpits? No. The smell is coming out of every pore. I'm sure I showered today. No, hang on – that was yesterday. I swam at a pool party yesterday. Surely that counts as a bath? Perhaps it was the day before, when I started this drug binge …

When did I start this drug binge?

Lights!

Why are they so bright?

Coming from outside. Hang on, someone is outside. Turn the lights off, I say to myself. I turn them off and freeze. More lights outside.

My heart is racing even faster now. It is pounding in my chest like a hammer. I go to the blinds and slowly lift them, looking outside. It's Sunday night, about 19:00.

I see the blue lights and the yellow-and-blue stripes of what is most definitely a cop van. The engine is idling, but I think I see a second one behind it. How many are there, exactly? Who let them into my secure complex? Did they follow my dealer and come in behind him? But my dealer last came yesterday? Someone let them in.

What are they doing there?

Did they see my light on?

Do they know?

I race to the spare room and crouch down low. I don't know how long I stay there in the dark. Hiding and watching. It feels like a few hours. Then the light goes on. A white light that will definitely show the cops that I am home.

'What are you doing?' A voice. My boyfriend's.

Panic.

'Turn off the light! They'll see me!'

He pulls a familiar face. One of disgust and dejection.

'What are you doing on the floor? Get up, man!'

'Cops! They're outside. You have to help me. They can't come in. They can't come in!' I am desperate.

He pauses for a minute, just staring down at me, on my knees, pleading with him.

'There are no cops.'

I look out the blinds. Stare for a minute. Then stand up in shame.

There is no one outside. The cops were never there.

It's the meth.

The meth has finally brought me to my knees.

'I just went a bit wild this once. I mean it. I didn't even take a lot. I won't touch it again. I promise.'

'Look at you,' he says, his face full of disgust. 'You are 35 years old. You've had everything on a silver platter, and you are wasting it. I wish I had half of what you have! And you are just throwing it all away.'

He is right. My money is running out. Two years ago, I had so much money saved in the bank. Now, I have no opportunities lined up, no savings left and little prospect of finding a job as a serious drug user with a very active nightlife.

'You need help!' he says, and walks out the room.

He has caught me red-handed. This is the end of the line. There is no hiding from him, or my problem, any more.

It's time to stop.

Well, not quite yet.

Perhaps it's time to come up with a plan instead.

My addict brain is always trying to come up with a plan for using. Tonight, it and I need to find a way to use the rest of the one gram of crystal meth I have in the little bag. The addict's brain is devious and fast.

I wait a bit. While he's in the bathroom, I find another empty meth bag and rush to fill it with white sugar. In an old, used bag, sugar and meth can look pretty much the same. I stand in the kitchen, waiting for him to come out the bathroom. My heart is thumping but my face is calm, ready to lie my way out of this again.

'Okay, you're right. I'm done with the drugs. I promise, I'm done,' I say. 'Look, I'm done! Come look. Watch me.'

I walk up to him, shaking the bag.

'Okay, what now?' He sighs, exhausted. He doesn't believe me.

'I am done with all this.' I take the bag of sugar and open it in front of him. 'I'm going to throw it all away and stop using tonight. Right now. Look! I'm throwing it all away. I don't need it any more. I'm done!'

I walk over to the sink and sprinkle it into the basin.

'Run the water,' he says. 'It must all go down the drain properly.'

I run it down the drain. 'See? I'm done!' I look at him with a proud face.

He nods in a way that shows me he isn't really convinced. 'I'm tired,' he says. He turns around and goes to bed.

I did it. Oh, thank God! I dodged this bullet. He's gone off to bed; I have the rest of the night back to myself.

I wait silently in the lounge, holding the last gram of the real crystal meth I hid. I am holding onto my freedom to do what I want. This is my meth and I am going to use it when I want and however I want.

I figure that in 10 minutes or so he'll be asleep, so I wait. Then I go back into the second bedroom, lock the door and take a hit. I cut myself a huge line.

Then, a paranoia sets in that is unlike any other I have ever had. I'm not seeing other people or things. No cops at the door, no evil faces on the walls.

This time, I am alone in my paranoia. It is just me. Me and my soul. Me and my being. Alone, with myself, I am rattling in confusion, pain and sadness. It feels like my soul is screaming at me. There is a primal scream of desperation in my head. I am unravelling. It feels like my soul is shaking me like a ragdoll.

Look what you've done, Costa!

Look how you've lied to and deceived everyone you love!

You staged a fake event to try to convince him! Look at yourself!

No one is shouting at me. I am shouting at myself.

Then, a window opens in my mind and a moment of extreme clarity comes over me.

The events of the night become clear. I realise I never wanted to deceive my boyfriend or hide the drugs, but that something has come over me that I cannot stop. The drugs are stronger than the urge to be real and honest. The drugs are talking, not me. The drugs are in control.

I see that moment for what it is. I see what I am doing, but can't stop myself. It's like there are two Costas: one who wants to be himself, honourable and drug free, and the other one, who has taken over and is in control. I watch this sinister second self do things, and see them for what they are – from a different perspective.

I realise that having lied about throwing away the drugs feels like an out-of-body experience. It is as if my *real self* is lifting out of this addict called Costa, and rising above him. I can see myself from above and am observing the entire situation.

In that moment, I watched myself lie, but I couldn't reach out to stop myself. I was powerless, and frozen. My second sinister self was in control and I watched and could do nothing about it.

I am terrified. I am no longer in control of who I am and what I am doing. That total loss of control is the horrific paranoia that is gripping me now. I sit in the spare bedroom and quickly cut myself another line. If I use more, perhaps this will all go away?

The opposite happens. The more I use, the more clarity I get that I am no longer in control. The more terror I feel.

I watch myself self-destruct as if I am a passenger in a speeding car with a reckless drunk driver. This clarity of my reality and terror is a miracle moment for me: a miracle of clear choices that I can see.

One path is to keep using.

I look around my apartment and realise, strangely, that I will lose all of it. All the money I had is already used up. Next up would be borrowing, lying, cheating and stealing, like other addicts I have heard of. I hear the voices in my own head.

What a great guy he was. Just be careful if he asks for money.
Nice guy – but have you heard …

This miracle moment delivers another choice. To stop using. These voices are clear. Voices I imagine to be my father's, or mother's, or sister's.

You are not made for this life.

Surely this isn't who you are?

There is no way you were raised to be this person.

Luckily for me, for a brief moment the fear becomes stronger than the drugs. With it, I feel a desperation that I never knew was humanly possible.

I get onto my knees and beg for my real life back. I am on my knees, physically, spiritually, mentally and emotionally. My real self wants out of this nightmare.

That is when I manage to find the words and the courage to say it.

'I will do *anything* in my power never to feel like this again.'

I am finally done.

THREE

THE LONG WALK TO FREEDOM

'If you want what I have, you have to do what I've done.'
— MY FUTURE SPONSOR

*A*nything! *I am prepared to do anything never to feel those
feelings again*, I kept telling myself.

I decided I needed to go to rehab. I mean, that's what all people
do when they want to stop drugs, right? I was now one of those
people. Only Dana had an idea of my drug use. Most others in
my life, my parents and non-using friends, had no clue I was even
using drugs, let alone that I was so far gone. They would soon get
a message that I was checking into rehab. Now wasn't the time
to think about their reactions. It was my mess, and I was going
to find a way out of it. I had a strong sense that I didn't want to
burden anyone else.

But first I had to go to work. I had to try to function. And that
I did, for the next few days.

I knew I had to take responsibility and action. Something kept
driving me, a pull that was so strong. I blocked everything else
out. I was in a mode, ready to do everything in my power never
to use drugs again.

I was given what is often referred to as the 'gift of desperation'.
That sounds like a crap gift: nobody ever wants to be desperate,
and certainly not to admit that they are. But this gift propelled
me in the right direction. Being desperate meant I was prepared
to go to great lengths to get better. The gift was a reminder of

where I was and where I never wanted to go again. Having that gift in my hand gave me so much strength and courage that it has defined my recovery.

There was a depressing comedown period I had to endure. For the few days after taking meth, the feelings of despair and emptiness are some of the worst feelings anyone can ever experience. A total emptiness of spirit. A hole in the soul is exposed and the pain is unbearable. *Only further using can fix that*, was a common thought that came into my mind.

But a new thought now entered my brain: *Hang on – no. Remember your last night of using.* A new pathway of thinking that was to save my life.

Three very confusing and terrifying days passed as I tried to keep going and went to work while I came up with a plan. I picked up my phone and called a government rehab centre I had heard about, finally ready to pack my bags and make my way over there for the next step in my life-saving process.

My enthusiasm was soon curbed when they insisted that I couldn't just come over and move in, and asked me to come for an interview instead. That really surprised me. I didn't know you had to be interviewed to go to rehab. People just walked through the doors, didn't they? Nobody does it accidentally. I had seen many celebrities escorted in dark glasses into rehab. Why couldn't I just walk in?

Fine!

I drove myself there, determined to nail the interview and be admitted.

'Well, um, Costa. Thank you for answering all the questions honestly. It's very clear that you need to be here.'

Duh! I thought. *Now let me in, please!*

I was desperate. It had been a few days. Cravings were setting in. I needed help badly. Just a few steps away was my bed, ready, with a six-week programme that would sort me out. Take me away from this hell.

'I am pleased to say we have a bed for you, Costa. But today is Thursday and tomorrow is Good Friday and, it being the Easter weekend, we can't admit you until we are fully staffed on Tuesday. Come back in four days' time, please.'

Was she fucking joking? My bags were packed and in my car!

Stunned, I walked out and sat in my car. Here I was, sitting outside what I thought was the only place that could save me, and they were closed for business. I was in Melville, a part of town where it was notoriously easy to score drugs, on the eve of a long weekend, with no work ahead of me – the perfect time to start using again. That is when the gift of desperation overrode every thought I had, and I took out my cell phone and called a friend of mine. Helga was a recovering alcoholic and part of a 12-step fellowship programme. I didn't know much about these programmes, but I did know that she'd had a problem once and had helped a few other people. She gave me a helpline number to call. I left a message on an automated answering service, and someone called me back within a few hours.

A very gentle man's voice on the other end of the line said, 'I once had a problem like yours. It's going to be okay. Why don't you come to one of our 12-step meetings? There's one tonight in Forest Town.'

'See you there,' I said.

And that night, I walked into my first meeting.

'Hi. My name is Costa and I am an addict.' Then, the tears. It was such a huge relief! Finally, the end of the drugs and the beginning of something new and hopeful. That very first night I was hugged by so many people, random strangers gave me their numbers to call if I needed help, and one guy even took me out for coffee to check in with me.

Best of all, these were people just like me. People called Mandy, Nicole, Joel, Lee, Heiki, Ray, Pieter and Murray.

Growing up, I used to love the sitcom *Cheers*. Ironically, it's set in a bar in Boston, a place you could go where everyone knew your name. Here I was, in a room where everybody got to hear my name and we all had the same objective: to help one another.

I heard in the preambles, which they read aloud at the beginning of every meeting, that the programme was a set of principles set out simply and in a way that was easy to follow. Why not give it a go? It was a public-holiday weekend, and all I wanted to do was go out and take drugs. Now I had a group of people who were just like me – some I even recognised from the nightclubs – prepared to do anything to help me *not* do that.

I went to one meeting, then another, and another. Tuesday came after the Easter weekend. I went to work, then to another meeting that night. I decided not to go back to the rehab centre and to give this programme a try instead. Something seemed to be working. Besides, it was free.

One person described it as a programme that was simple, but not easy, and said to me, 'How free do you want to be?' My gift of desperation came up again; I wanted freedom so badly!

The 12-step programme started out as a set of suggestions. I liked the word 'suggestions'. They weren't orders – they came from people who were nudging me in a certain direction. At my first meeting, the people there told me to take all the suggestions I was given. So I did. These suggestions formed the foundation of my recovery and life as it is today. They suggested I go to the meetings. So, I went. Here, I met a community of people who were all incredibly individual. They came across as super brave, a little crazy, some creative, some wild, some gentle. *A little bit of me in each one of them*, I thought.

Hang on – they were all heavy-using druggies. People who had probably used even more than I had, for many more years. It was crazy to think that we were all sitting around, now, trying to make better lives for ourselves. I had the chance to hang out with the people like me – people who were all trying to do the same thing.

They suggested 90 meetings in 90 days. So I went. This hard-wired the programme into my daily life and headspace. I had a place to go to every night – pretty handy, when the nights were when I wanted to go out. I used to drive around looking to do lines; now we sat in circles, talking about how never to do lines again.

They suggested I reach out and meet new people who didn't do drugs, and take their numbers. Within a few days, I had more numbers in my phone belonging to people who didn't want me to use drugs than numbers of those with whom I'd ever used. I would never need to be alone.

They suggested I offer to wash the coffee cups at the end of meetings. So I did. That was the start of humility lessons.

They suggested I get a sponsor and do the steps. The key to my freedom lay in that process (more about that later).

They suggested I actually use my sponsor. So I called him daily. This started some accountability training.

They told me to do service. So I started serving on some committees, giving back and completing the circle.

They suggested I buy their literature. So I did; I always had a handy guidebook for many situations.

They suggested I put nothing before my recovery. So I didn't. Receiving the gift of desperation meant throwing myself entirely into the programme. I even got the name 'Captain Recovery' from a few.

After a couple of months, a huge relief came over me. I found myself convinced that this was going to work for the rest of my life. I also realised that this whole programme was a master trick, and that two of the biggest tricks were working their magic on me. Firstly, the suggestions are more than that. They are more like strict rules, tried and tested ways that millions before me have used to clean up – just packaged in a lighter, subtler, more palatable way. Brilliant! Had I been given rules at my first meeting, rather than suggestions, I would have run for the hills.

And secondly: this was actually a spiritual programme, all about the Big Man above. Yes, Him.

The G-word freaked me out. It meant religion and layers of dogma to me. I had prayed to Him often as a little boy to help me with the taunting at school, but the bullying had continued. I had asked for my feelings for other men to be explained, but had got smacked down in Athens. That word brought up feelings of guilt. It was a constant reminder of the concept of sin and resulting punishment, particularly for people like me – gay, and now a recent drug addict.

I remembered my gran's prayer books and their drawings of heaven and hell. Hell was represented much like a Goya painting. Evil men dripping with blood, long-horned rams, and Satan peering at the scene. Hell is where gay men like me were headed. I felt the church had rejected me, and had even got word of this from the 'Pope' himself in Athens. My concept of God was so messed up in my head when I came into recovery.

Now, I was hearing the G-word non-stop, along with other fluffy words like 'Higher Power' and 'the Universe'. They all repelled me. God was something outside of me. An enemy, almost. A punisher. Someone I just didn't understand, and quite frankly didn't want to understand at that stage.

But the programme is very cleverly devised. It eased me into the concept of God, gently and slowly. I was advised to find a concept of a Higher Power that worked for me. The only important thing was that this power was meant to be greater than me. One guy chose Formula 1 racing as his Higher Power. To him, the entire sport enthralled him and felt greater than himself. I now had to choose my own concept. Not cars, though. That was taken.

Having a clearer mind after some days of abstinence, I would start waking up earlier. I found it very relaxing to sit on my couch and watch the sun come up. In the meeting rooms of recovery, a friend of mine, Geoff, calls it 'the God moment', the moment when the fiery African sun turns the sky blood red at the horizon then comes up. Once, I was watching this happen when a bird came into my view. It landed on the deck and I watched it walk about, looking for something. It then flew up into the sky, into the sunrise: free, peaceful, creative and beautiful. I had found my Higher Power: birds.

Birds were a part of nature. Something much greater than myself. They had freedom, grace and beauty. They were everywhere, gentle and full of songs.

My friend Andrea told me once that Carl Jung believed that addiction could only really be dealt with by replacing it with a spiritual awakening of some sort. Over time, and through the programme, my concept of a Higher Power evolved and developed into what it is today. It is a deeply personal relationship. I feel I have a strong connection with myself and my Higher Power. This allows me to remember my true spirit and essence always, and to accept my life as it is – full of serenity, opportunity and love. My Higher Power saved my life, and I am forever grateful to my programme for helping me get there.

Birds still follow me everywhere. They arrive to keep me

company when I feel sad. They fly in front of my car to remind me to slow down. They drop feathers on my path to show me support.

As time goes by, if you follow the programme it leads to a spiritual awakening – not suddenly, but slowly. It is something that happens daily, incrementally and gently over time.

If you told me while I was still using that, one day in early recovery I would be sitting with a bunch of addicts talking about my Higher Power, I would have run a mile. But I sat in those meetings, and continued with them, and am so glad I did.

In the programme's basic text is a part that talks about how one addict is best equipped to help another. It is in the programme that I not only learnt how to deal with and love the people who were already in my life, but also met people who would shape my life in the most loving way.

'Hi, I'm Joanne, and I have a feeling we are going to be best friends,' she said in a husky voice, and gave me a huge, warm hug.

I was sitting quietly in a circle of people, listening and minding my own business. The first 30 days of my recovery had passed and, as usual, I had left work and come to a meeting, like I did every night. Most often, I would sit inside and wait for a meeting to start. Everyone outside was smoking, which would get up my nose as I had stopped a year earlier. It also helped to calm me while I waited for the meeting to start. Thirty minutes into the meeting, most were ready for the break – to have another cigarette, of course. I would head straight for the coffee and biscuits. But this time, before I could walk away from my chair I found myself in a huge embrace with a complete stranger. And that is how the fellowship worked. It is a custom that we don't shake

Joanne and I.

hands, but rather hug. And it's these hugs that, in the past 30 days, I'd been taking a little time to get used to.

Active addiction disconnected me from people – and clearly from myself, too. Now, I'd been thrust into what felt like deeply intimate French kissing. A warm hug means touching someone's heart area physically, along with feeling the warmth of their hands touching your back. A little pat on the back also makes you feel supported. It's a comforting feeling that we got used to when we were cuddled as children.

One minute I was in my own little world, eyeing out the biscuits, planning how I was going to make a dash to get to them first, and the next I was in a strong embrace with a person who had decided, without getting my opinion, that we were going to be best friends. (She was right!)

That night, we exchanged numbers – as all good recovering

addicts do – and the very next weekend, we met for coffee – as all good recovering addicts do. In our one hour of having coffee, I shared more with her than I had shared with most people in my entire life, and so did she. Our stories made it easy to relate to each other, and the programme was the glue. Over the years, Joanne has helped me to laugh at myself. She never takes herself too seriously and has helped me lighten up. From her, I get a feeling I hadn't felt from the friends in my life for many years: a deep sense of unconditional love. This was something only my sister, parents or cousins would be expected to give me. Not a friend, I thought. It's thanks to Joanne, the programme and many other new friends that I realised that unconditional love is possible from such friendships. A foundation was being laid for me to try to be that kind of friend to others – that same kind of person.

I'd heard that addiction is a shame-based disease – that shame drives addictive behaviours. Shame is something that has followed me around my whole life. Shame about how my bullies made me feel, about never being heard or seen for who I was. Shame about my homosexuality. Shame about my drug use and the destruction it wreaked.

It was time to hand back the shame. The way to do this is through self-acceptance. Accepting who I was felt impossible in the beginning, but so much about the programme leads to self-acceptance.

Each day, I would talk about being gay in the meetings. Not once was I ever judged. Not once did it come up as something that wasn't accepted. Most times, it was celebrated. Where once I couldn't be myself in many environments – the real me, the exposed me – now I could, in a 12-step programme room where there was no judgement. Self-acceptance in a diverse community that had only a few other gay men!

In early recovery, I often felt like a total failure. I had blown so many chances, and lost a ton of money. I had missed out on many productive years. But I'd always get a trademark hug from a ton of people at the start of a meeting, and then there was the meeting itself. As my sponsor said, 'You never leave a meeting feeling worse than when you arrived.' I would often leave having forgotten about my failures, with some self-acceptance and less shame about it all.

In these meetings, there is an environment not seen in the outside world: there is no cross-talk. This means that no one is allowed to talk while you are talking. Even better, no one is allowed to advise anyone about how to do anything. All you do is share what is going on for you. Night after night, I sat in a room full of people, each of us respectfully letting the other be heard. I needed to be heard. For once in my life, I was. Watching them all nod while I was speaking, I realised it: I was home.

From my early days of bullying, I'd grown up fearing men and the power they could have over me. In the programme, I watched grown men cry, hug me, call me, counsel me and console me. I felt accepted by men. They were not any different from me. This made self-acceptance easier. When you are being bullied, you constantly think you have done something wrong – that it is *you* who needs to change. After forming strong bonds with adult men based on honesty and love, I realised I was fine just the way I was.

I felt incredible shame about having been raped all those years ago. I was made to feel filthy, worthless and powerless. It was time to hand back that shame, and the programme nurtured this process. I started talking honestly in a few group meetings about the rape, and got a lot of support. Then, my amazing friend Joanne jumped in.

'It's time to hand over the shame, Popalopoulos,' she said,

using the affectionate name she'd given me, her crazy Greek friend. 'We are finally going to report it to the police.'

Ten years after the fact, I was led into my local police station by a dear friend, who had taken over the situation. She spoke to the station commander and, before I knew it, I was sitting at a desk with a large, matronly policewoman with a soft, beautiful face, holding a pen.

'Tell me what happened, Costa. It's okay,' she said, with a huge smile and loving eyes.

'Hi, my name is Sarah, and I may perhaps be an addict,' the beautiful blonde girl sitting next to me said. She wore a simple outfit with pumps, and sat in a very ladylike way. This was during my first 30 days. I had been to a few meetings, and heard a few people's stories. After hearing Sarah share, I knew I needed to approach her during the break and tell her something.

I went up to her and introduced myself to her with a hug. 'Sarah, my dear,' I said, 'you *are* an addict.'

Her eyes widened and she let out her trademark infectious laugh as she realised that someone had seen through her mask and called her out on her behaviour. An hour before, she'd been a complete stranger, and now I was telling her about something very personal I had observed. This is what the programme did: it had filtered out the bullshit from all our lives. We could spot it in one another. Sarah became a loving friend, and we would come to share a bond that was inherently based on what most friendships should be based on: accountability. It would not just be about the good times and the fun coffee dates – and there are tons of those – but also about being accountable to each other and ourselves. I was finally owning up for the shit that was mine, and doing something about it.

172

For this reason, I decided not to tell my parents I was in recovery. I'd got myself into this mess, and wanted to get myself out of it. I thought that, if I told them, they would be concerned and worried about whether it would all work out. They didn't need that burden. I decided to tell them when I'd been clean for six months. That way, I could prove it was working, and there'd be nothing for them to worry about.

I needed to dodge them a lot in those six months, as I went to meetings on most days. But it wasn't impossible: I would go for dinner on a Thursday and miss a meeting. I would make up that meeting by going to two on a Saturday. I was determined to get seven meetings done in seven days – every week!

When I finally did tell them, I came clean about everything. No more secrets. I'd held myself accountable and was solving my adult problem in a very adult way. It worked: they were left with a sense that I had a handle on things, and became super supportive of this new process in my life. Of course – they were my loving parents.

'Hi, my name is Costa. Will you please be my sponsor?'

There I stood, in front of a tall, lanky man, 10 years my junior, humbly asking him to help me. I had never spoken to him before. He was a complete stranger and, in that moment, I had surrendered a part of myself. I stood before him exposed and vulnerable. How did I manage that? Call it the gift of desperation. But I did as had been suggested: I'd been told to find a sponsor and given a very simple instruction to find someone who had something that I wanted.

It was a Tuesday night meeting. I had found a room that would soon be my home group. Not because my sponsor would be there, but because this meeting was different. It was held in a stone church hall with a wonderful rose garden. The room's wooden floors and floral, floor-length curtains made it look and feel elegant. It was steeped in history, having been built in 1946, and its upmarket qualities made me feel special – a small comfort in the fearful and strange first days of recovery.

This meeting was oddly called the 'bells' meeting. After the first 15 minutes, I realised why.

Every Tuesday night, certain members of the parish would get together to practise ringing the bells for the church. Normally, they would ring out on a Sunday to signify the start of a sermon, but on Tuesday nights, these people would pull on ropes. Five storeys up, the church's large brass bells, made in 1946, would start to ring out. Incredibly loudly. They were so loud, in fact, that for much of the time they'd be ringing you couldn't hear what people were saying. The bells would irritate many, but I found them a comfort. Their noise and interruption were welcome. They would come into my ears and hijack my brain. For those minutes, my messy head would hear something even louder than the inner voices of self-loathing and doubt.

Often, the parish members would train new members on the bells on Tuesday nights. As such, the bells were often out of synch. I would picture the poor newbie pulling on the rope for the first time, being hoisted right off his feet, and see his panicked look when he realised he was the only person who was off the beat. I imagined the other bell-ringers trying to pull him back down, and him bumping them a little, and their bells losing their rhythm too. A cacophony of maddening bells would sometimes ring out for over 20 minutes, but this random and irregular noise made my brain feel a little more at peace. There was something out there crazier than me; I was not alone in my muddled mess of a life. And these bells were a comfort at my newly self-appointed

Tuesday night home group.

Here I now stood, in front of a man I knew nothing about, asking him to be my sponsor. Asking him for help. I was admitting I could not do it alone and trusting that someone else knew better. I had trust that this was the right person, because I'd been given some advice: 'Find someone who has something that you want,' and, 'Go with your gut.' My gut told me that Riaan could be trusted, and he had serenity in his life – I wanted that.

'Of course,' he said. 'I will be your sponsor.'

'Oh, okay.' I shuffled in front of him. 'What do we do next?' I asked.

'Take my number first. I want you to call me every day at the same time until I tell you to stop.'

'Okay.'

That seemed strange, but I didn't question it and took his number down.

'Tell me how you are feeling when you call me each day,' Riaan said.

So, I have to call this complete stranger and tell him how I feel once a day? I thought. But I actually got excited about it. I felt a loving pull towards him. Here was someone who genuinely wanted to hear how I was feeling, and who didn't even know me. I felt so lucky that someone like that existed. *This might just work*, I thought.

'Okay, cool! I can do that. Thanks, Riaan,' I said, and walked out of the room towards my car.

In the programme, we start out as a group of total strangers who try to help one another. It's about helping another person. Who cares about the details? The selfless help is what matters most.

Riaan had forgotten one primary detail. 'Hey, wait!' he called out to me when I was almost out of earshot. 'What's your name?'

'Yiayia, I'm dying for a hit of crystal meth.'

'Hey Dad, I can't remember who I hooked up with a few weeks before I stopped using.'

Statements like these are enough to drive a parent to prescription tranquilisers. They are loaded with the horror and desperation of active addiction. They are not meant for the general public, either.

And that is one of the biggest reasons why I loved going to recovery meetings. I am not the only one who talks like that. I am also not judged for what comes out of my mouth.

People got me in these meetings. They got how I can finish a meeting with top business executives and leave the room craving a line of cocaine. They got how, while driving home in traffic, I would think how four strong headache tablets and a double whisky would give me the perfect buzz to start off the evening. How sometimes, with no warning, I got the taste of crystal meth on my tongue.

'No, Mom. I'm not about to relapse. I just need to tell another addict.'

I'd do so, and the feelings would go away.

Many years later, people remark, 'You didn't go to rehab?' But I'd found something that worked for me. With hindsight, rehab may have been an easier ride at the beginning. But I decided to go to work every day and to a meeting every night. Perhaps it was this tough start to my recovery that made it stronger? All I knew was that there was a force driving me to those meetings after work every night.

But another force started developing too: a dark one that would get me in its grip and nearly destroy all the hard work I'd put into recovery.

'The urge to use has lifted today,' said Joanne, sharing at a recovery meeting.

What the fuck is that about? I thought, feeling myself fill with jealousy. It was time to have a talk with her during the break.

Being one of the few who didn't smoke, I was always annoyed during the breaks. Catching some fresh air was impossible, given the 50 or so smokers outside. Pushing through the smoke clouds, I found Joanne and walked up to her.

'What a load of crap. The urge to use has been lifted? How can that be, Jo? I've been thinking about using all day, all week. I'm six months clean and feel no better. You're bugging me!' I said to her.

She was, indeed, irritating me, but she also knew me as a close friend and could see exactly where I was coming from. She could tell that my angst was not directed at her, but at another issue that was becoming more and more clear.

'You go to meetings, right?' she said. 'You have a sponsor and do step work? You pray every day?' she asked about my programme.

'Yes, yes, yes – I am doing it all. Taking every bloody suggestion!' I shouted back in frustration.

Joanne was the one who had given me the name 'Captain Recovery' for being so diligent about my programme and the way I approached recovery. But on this night, I felt like my cape was in shreds and my superpowers were diminishing.

'I've told you before, and I'm telling you again. Stop messing around and go and see Dr P,' she said, raising her voice.

I grunted and went back into the meeting. I knew she was right. That name had come up again and again. Many I knew in recovery had experienced the magic of Dr P, but I refused to listen.

'I can do this recovery thing myself, with the help of this

programme,' I would stubbornly say. But despite all my best efforts, six months down the line I was clean but hostile. Sober but miserable. I was doing the recovery work, but had no energy left for anything or anyone. I had a new community of loving friends, but was always angry. I was working through the emotional stuff, but became negative about life easily. Something was up.

'You're depressed,' Dr P, my new psychiatrist, said very seriously. 'How have you managed to stay clean like this for so long?'

His question was a valid one. I was bloody miserable. Life plodded on and on with a rhythm that felt gloomy and sad. Most days in meetings I would hear other addicts talk about their recovery unfolding beautifully and their lives brightening up, but for me that was not the case. Things were not getting better. Things were sullen and sometimes dark, and often very sad.

'Listening to your life story, I can see you have had many episodes of depression, particularly when you were young.'

He was right. I remember being very sad at times as a child. These were counteracted by the times when I was happy, loved and content as well. Life for me was a normal cycle of very sad times and very happy times.

I am no psychiatrist or recovery specialist, but my personal experience leads me to believe that I must have developed many of my compulsions and addictions as a way to cope with my underlying depression. These had evolved as I'd got older, until I was a recovering alcoholic and addict, sitting in a chair at the famous Dr P – famous in recovery circles in Johannesburg, as he had treated so many of the friends I had made in the past six months.

'What are your thoughts about me putting you on medication?'

asked Dr P. I liked the way he suggested it, as if to feel me out. I liked suggestions. It was certainly a good way of bringing it up, as I had been sceptical in the past about head meds. *Therapia* is not for us Greeks – let alone *Xapia* (pills)! Mental illness was not something I wanted to think about. *Only sick people take head meds*, I thought. But this time, I knew I was the one who was sick. Things were clearly not normal, and I was suffering, despite the hard work Captain Recovery was putting in.

Only those who have experienced depression can tell you what it feels like. I liked an analogy I'd heard that referred to it as the fog. It comes in quietly, and settles. It clouds everything out. It's dense and doesn't shift easily. You can see some of the light coming through, and it reaches you, but it certainly doesn't feel like it is shining upon you. The fog makes it hard to think and get your bearings. It's cold. No one likes to sit in the fog alone.

The fog is so difficult to explain to those who don't understand depression – particularly when I tried explaining that I would rather be dead! Wanting your own death is the dramatic result of a very painful feeling of sadness. It's not that I wanted to die. It's just that I'd rather not be alive. When I was like that, I wished I could just blink and everything would end – like that moment you see the last flash as you turn off the TV with your remote.

It's not like you're planning on where to buy a gun or how to hang a rope on a high beam. It's just a general feeling of wanting to go for a long sleep. A very, very long sleep. One that lasts forever, perhaps.

'You need a holiday!' said some colleagues.

'Have a long, hot bath!' was the advice of a friend's mother.

'Think positive thoughts!' said a crystal-wielding, dream-catcher-earringed, hippie friend.

'Just pray!' others would say.

'It's sugar, you have to stop sugar!' said some longevity and health magazines.

All these had great intentions, but when you are depressed nothing seems to work.

The analogy I often use to describe how it feels to be depressed is winning the lottery. If you told me I had won $20 million, the first thought that would go through my mind is the effort it would take to find the ticket and the obsession with where I'd hidden it. Once I'd found the ticket, I would probably have to endure some long interview process with the lottery authorities, who would no doubt make me engage with the tax authorities. That would involve getting a tax consultant of some form. I would have to negotiate about their fees, as I often find them exorbitant. Then, I would have to find an outfit for the press photo opportunity. But then perhaps I would want to stay anonymous. Would they let me? The effort would then revolve around putting together a list of the people I would tell. Who could I trust? Who would be left out? What if it got out? How would I manage their comments, judgements, expectations and feelings about my having won $20 million?

Being depressed robbed me of finding joy, in the lottery analogy. Nothing is light in depression. Nothing is easy. Everything feels like a colossal and unhappy effort. Medication was prescribed for me for the first time in 2007, and I am happy to say it changed my life.

But talking about the medication didn't come without its judgements from others. Some people commented that I was substituting one drug for another: a cruel comment that I would often counter with, 'Well, if that is the case, then why did I wait four weeks for the meds to kick in?' I never waited more than 30 seconds for the cocaine to work, a few minutes for alcohol. Now,

I was taking this tiny white tablet each morning and waiting for four weeks for something to happen.

'Yes, but don't the meds change your personality? Numb you by taking out the highs and the lows?' This is another invasive and insensitive comment I would hear all the time. Certainly, some meds like heavy tranquilisers do exist, and some people need them for mental health issues they have. I am not here to comment on those.

My medication had a profound effect on me. It made me feel normal again. I started to have normal reactions to life. When I was supposed to be sad, I was sad. When things looked good, I was positive. This is how I knew my life was meant to be. There were also so many more hours in the day, once the meds had started working. I used to spend so much time worrying about events and how they were going to affect me, or how I needed to control them, that most of the day was taken up with angst. The meds opened my mind to a new clarity. A balance came back into my life. Things felt a little more possible than they used to.

Over the years, I have come to take the meds for granted, but a trip to Greece made me appreciate them so much more. In early recovery, and before medication, I had gone to Greece on a family trip and remember not being in the best of moods. My cousin Mia referred to me as 'the drip': I would always want to go home early, or sleep late.

I remember seeing litter everywhere, graffiti on the walls and the sad state of a population that was going through a terrible economic crisis. 'You are in Greece, Costa!' I would keep reminding myself. 'Perk up, this is great!' But I would avoid people and read instead – and stay away from children in particular, who tended to make so much noise.

Many years later, I went back to Greece. The crisis had

deepened so much, and poverty and strife were a part of every-day life for Greeks. I braced myself for some hard interactions and tough scenes. But something felt strange. People were being nice to me. Shop assistants were friendly; there was less litter and graffiti around.

We were travelling as a family and I would bring up the positivity and new changes I was noticing, but they would tell me I was wrong – that, in fact, things may even have got worse. That's when I realised that it was me who was different.

A few years of stability later, I tried to self-medicate and slowly weaned myself off the medication. I was feeling fine, confident that I was doing the right thing. What I soon realised is that the real reason I was feeling fine was because I was on the medication. Weaning myself off worked for a few weeks, and then a deep depression set in that caught me by surprise. Worse, Dr P had left the country and I needed to find a new psychiatrist. Enter the lovely Dr K, a super-bright young woman I have come to love over the years for her brutal honesty, impeccable care and thorough knowledge of my mind and me. Together, we have tinkered with medication and doses, and found a perfect balance that has resulted in many years of stability and growth in me as an individual.

Depression is a thief. It robbed me of an integral part of who I am: my outgoing and positive nature. It is partly thanks to medication that I feel as good as I do today.

But the medication isn't the only factor. It forms part of a greater set of activities and things I call my daily vitamins: spiritual work, sleep, diet, writing, my 12-step programme, creative exercises like collaging and vision boards, quiet time, and meditation.

One other thing was to become part of my daily life, however – the thing that has been the single biggest factor in changing my depressive state and turning my life around. It is the one thing I'd dreaded for most of my life. The word this whisky-drinking, Marlboro-smoking Greek guy never dared to utter: exercise!

ONE BLOCK

'Trexa trexa! Tha se piaso me tin pantofla
(*Run, run! I will catch you and hit you with this slipper*).'

— YIAYIA

Stopping drugs and alcohol (and smoking) has a profound impact on the way you spend your time. Gone are the wasted hours of using and partying, and the long days of sleeping. A whole new world opens up, one in which you wake up as the sun rises – every day of the week. You are also wide awake when you are up. All these hours come back into your life. The day is filled with time. Time for what? This is where something new started to creep into my life.

Exercise! The word alone would make me recoil in disgust. All that effort and exertion and energy was something I scorned on a daily basis.

I'm Greek. We exercise by throwing dice onto a backgammon board and lifting espresso cups.

Of course, I knew exercise was good for me. But so were many other things in the old days, like diet and restful sleep, and I'd scorned those too. In addition to time, something else becomes available in abundance when you're in recovery. Energy! One day, this energy led to a groundbreaking moment that was to change my life forever.

My boyfriend Dana had started running. He used to be a good runner in his youth and had decided to take it up again to get fit.

He was over 40 and looking for ways to get onto a healthier path while he was still young enough to do so. He was training for the gruelling 89 km Comrades Marathon that takes place every winter. Training for this race, for those with an already strong base of running, takes about eight months of almost daily running.

On most weekends, he would get up before me and head out for his daily run. I would stir a little and wait for him to leave before cracking a smile to myself. How silly he was wasting his time with all this running, I would think.

But one morning, a madness came over me.

'I'm coming running with you,' I said to him.

'Go back to sleep, Cos,' he said.

'No, really. Wait for me. I won't be a minute.'

He rolled his eyes

Oh shit! What did I just sign up for? was my immediate thought.

What shoes do I wear? I rummaged in the cupboard and found a pair of old-fashioned sneakers – the kind that worked well on a dancefloor and had got me through many all-nighters.

These puppies will do just great, I thought.

'Time for some carbo-loading,' I said to him.

'You must be joking, right?' he answered. 'You carbo-load a day or two before a race. This is an early morning training run. Get moving or I'm leaving.'

I quickly drank some juice, then came up with another pre-run delay tactic.

'Time to stretch. It's been a long time since I last ran and I don't want to hurt anything.' This was a desperate plea for him to let me off the hook. Surely it would work.

'You stretch *after* a run, and besides, you've never run before. I'm leaving.' He headed for the door.

It was now or never: get up off the kitchen bar stool and venture out into the uncertain terrain of body movement and exercise, or stay here, watch him leave and head back to bed.

I got up and followed him out the door. We headed down the hill. He mentioned that we would start by going around the block. My heart started pounding, but my legs were strong. I could feel the air rushing on my face, which was a new sensation so early in the morning. Halfway around the block I started to tire, and we slowed down. It was a tough moment: I wanted to give up, but my partner pushed me along with encouragement.

'Come on, Cos. We're warming up,' he said.

I must have heard wrong. 'Warming up' meant things had not even started. I was nearing the peak of my ability. I was dying. I ignored his comment, put my head down and pushed hard. I picked up the pace; I was going to do this. I had finally found a spring in my step. I was bouncing to great new heights.

'Stop shuffling your feet. Pick them up,' he said. Okay, so maybe I wasn't pushing as hard as I thought. But yikes, it was hurting.

We came around to the end of the block and were back near our gate. I ran towards it. We were done! Relief at last.

I noticed Dana had not followed me. He had stopped, and was shouting at me. 'Turn around, we've only done one block!'

I was very confused. We had completed our run for the day, had we not?

'You go on. I'm done.'

He left, continuing the run he had planned. I went into the apartment and ran a hot bath. I soaked my tired legs in the warm water, with a large grin on my face. *I have started running*, I thought.

I washed, dried myself, and jumped into bed. I was floating on a high. I lay there, dreamy-eyed, contemplating what had just happened. I had officially completed my first training run. I was so proud of myself. I treated myself to a catnap, as I felt super tired. I had officially run one entire large block.

I had once measured the distance around the block, but had forgotten what it was. So, the next day I drove my car around it. It had two little hills in it. I eagerly looked at my odometer. It measured 700 m!

My incredible achievement was a whole 700 m. I know what you're thinking. You'd cover 700 m walking around the office in a day. But to me, it represented so much more. Sitting in my car at the 700 m mark outside our gate, I named this my one-block moment. Looking at the gate, I started thinking about these words. Something profound started to surface.

The number one is important to me. I have come to realise more and more that I live in a binary world. By way of example, I'm either using drugs, or I'm not. Working on my recovery, or not. Moving towards success, or not. My life has been character-ised by a series of ones and zeroes. I was either going to stay in bed that day, or go running.

In my case, a block was a very short 700 m, a training session that almost everybody would laugh at. But I realised that a block represented more than a unit of measurement. A block, I thought, was one part of something. Most often, a block is part of some-thing much bigger. Building blocks came to mind. I thought of LEGO, which I loved as a kid. You never played with just one block – you always built something bigger. You also never left one block lying around, alone. It was always attached to another block. It *needed* other blocks

I had created my first block. What would happen next in the LEGO of my life?

I didn't think much about the run the next day, but a few days later I woke up wondering what it would feel like to run one block again. I mean, I had one LEGO block lying around, waiting to be used. So, that Saturday I woke up at the same time as my partner and asked if I could join him on his morning run.

'What? I'm happy for you, but please, this time, can you pick up the pace?'

I didn't blame him for being impatient. Running at snail's pace when you are well on track to an ultramarathon can't be pleasant.

'Let's do this!' I sounded all pumped and ready to take this on. I selected a vest that pulled really tight over my belly. I was now in rather unhealthy shape: two very skinny legs and a growing middle section. Toothpicks for arms, and no shoulders. I was no cover boy, with my belly showing too prominently and my seriously out-of-fashion running-style shorts.

Off we headed. Again, I found myself struggling on the two hills. But I pushed as hard as I could.

'Oh no, where are you going?' shouted Dana.

'I'm done!'

And I was. I went home again. I lay in the bath, soothing my tired legs, thinking *I have officially run twice in one week*. The scale of the achievement was huge. I was now a twice-a-week runner. That felt insane and unnatural. 'Natural' was running to the shops to get chocolate. 'Natural' was dancing all night. This was totally out of character. What the hell was I doing? Why did I feel so awesome? Perhaps I could do this again, twice, next week. Just repeat what I had done. *Nothing new, just a continuation of my brilliance of this week*, I thought.

Something interesting happened on the second run I did that following week. I got to the end of the block and thought, *Maybe you can run a second block. Try it, even if you walk it.* Much to my surprise and glee, I ran (shuffled) most of it. And there I had it. A 100 per cent improvement on my previous run – 100 per cent! I'd only ever got 100 per cent finishing a bottle of beer in the past.

One block had led to two. I had always heard that exercise done repetitively would result in fitness and, naturally, an increase in exercise volume. I'd never experienced this with my own body, though. Never had I felt my own legs experience it. Never had I felt something so viscerally. I had doubled what I had done the week before. It was in my bones, a cumulative effect beating inside me with every sore twitch of my muscles.

The following week, I decided to run one block again – three times. What happened was that I ran a double block on all three occasions, more than doubling the previous week's achievements.

'So, how many kilometres did you run this week?' my partner asked.

'I ran 4.2 km,' I told him. 'I'm so bloody happy with myself. I'm a runner now.' I felt like I was part of an elite group of humans who take their bodies to a new limit of perfection. I was now that guy. 'How many did you run?' I asked, keen to compare our achievements.

'I did 84 km.'

Fuck!

At that moment, I galvanised my next motivational concept.

'I'm a runner,' I said proudly.

I was sitting at a dinner table having partnered my best friend Joanne to a work function she'd invited me to, and we'd been seated with some of her suppliers. A handsome man next to me had asked me what I enjoyed doing. I loved that question. It was so much more informative than the standard 'What do you do for a living?' He was in his late 20s, and looked particularly fit. I continued the conversation. 'You look like you work out too.

What do you enjoy doing?'

'Oh, I'm quite active,' was his response.

Quite active? I thought, detecting a touch of humility in his bashful response. 'Cool. What's the most active thing you've ever done?' He was a runner for sure, I thought. Perhaps a judo guy of sorts. Hang on – he could be one of those off-road bikers who ride for a few days in the desert.

'Last year, I summited Mount Everest,' he said.

I was sitting next to Lance Metz – at the time, the youngest South African ever to have climbed Mount Everest.

'That's, um … okay, cool!' I stumbled. At just that moment, the main course was served. I mean, what else can you say? 'Oh, I've done that before,' or 'My cousin did that last week'?

That moment blindsided me. I was sitting next to a super-human. He had achieved the most gruelling and stressful of activities, accomplished a feat that few on this planet have ever accomplished. His mother was sitting at the table opposite me. I imagined the pride she felt, having such a superhuman son.

Imagine her sitting with my mother and a few of her friends over tea and baklava.

'My Costa is very good at marketing,' was something my mother loved to say to her friends.

'My Spiro has a speedboat of his own on the Vaal River,' one of my mother's friends would competitively chirp.

A Greek mother's self-worth is intimately tied to her son's achievements. Our Greek mothers worked hard to raise us. With all the sun they allowed to shine on us, they were only too happy to brag to their friends that the sun also shone out of our asses.

Enter Mrs Metz. 'My Lance climbed Mount Everest.'

Silence. No Greek mother could top that – not even my own mother's blind faith in her son's ability to change the marketing landscape of our planet with his stellar ideas.

At that stage, Lance was training to be the first South African to summit another 8 000 m peak called Cho Oyu without the use of oxygen, he went on to tell me after main course. This was too much. Not only was it difficult to concentrate sitting next to a man that good-looking, but I just could not comprehend this kind of effort. It was hard enough to endure months of training, let alone to go through the entire climb surrounded by the thinnest air on our planet.

There is a fine line between being inspired by someone and being made to feel worthless by their stellar achievements. That evening, I felt both. We live in an age of mega-achievement. It's all around us. Superbly well-trained athletes bombard our television screens. Championships in every sport fill arenas and social media for us to consume. Most of it is very entertaining to watch – but, on another level, it represents a level very few of us will ever achieve.

Being all around us, this achievement almost seems available to us all. So, as a man, I wanted a piece of that. Sitting next to Lance, I knew I wanted what he had. I wanted to try to get close to it in my own life, at least.

The problem was that, since my early teens, I'd done little or nothing to get fit. I was the guy who'd sat at a coffee shop admiring the view while 40 other exchange students had hiked down the Grand Canyon when I was in the US at 18. Backgammon was my sport of choice as an adult. It went very well with cigarettes. *I'm Greek – that's what we do*, I told myself.

Once or twice, with the coming of the first flowers of spring, I got some inspiration and tried a gym class or a walk. That would last a few hours, then I'd be back to my partying ways. Nothing I had done in the past had succeeded. Any intentions I'd had to

get fit had failed to even start. Fitness took effort and determination. Mostly, it looked like something that was just too great to
achieve. Most people around me also battled with this stalling,
this bankrupt inspiration, whenever they tried to get fit.

Tonight, at this fancy dinner, I finally realised why. It was
because of guys like Lance Metz! I stubbornly decided that aiming high was the problem. How the hell do you even compare to
a man like this? Where do you even start to feel good about yourself and your own fitness goals? Sorry, Superman, but sitting next
to you I felt only daunted. My ego smashed, I felt I had no chance
of taking my fitness anywhere great.

I had to do it differently this time if it was going to work.

Why not aim low? Let me try that. If I aimed low, I reckoned,
I would always achieve my goals. And so, I did. I kept my goals
small and manageable. What was more important to me was
achieving the goal – not necessarily the extent, height, distance,
weight, or length of the goal.

Achieving my weekly goals became my mission. Sure, I knew
I was setting them quite low, but I focused on achieving them
rather than on any judgements that arose in my own head. This
only worked properly when I accessed two different sides of my
ego and behaved in two different ways. First, I had to suppress the
side of my ego that was my critic. The side that would scoff at
the low level of some of my goals. I had to ignore him. And I did.
Second, I had to puff up my ego and bask in the glory of achieving and celebrating my goals. We are ego-driven, I thought; by
stroking this side of my ego when I attained a goal, I was making
myself feel good.

And here, the secret to my success began to bubble up. I realised that, if it felt good, I would do it again. If it felt good, I
would look at myself differently. Perhaps I would look at myself

as having more potential – with more self-love, even.

I was not achieving any amazing results – I knew that. But I was a man who constantly reached his goals. I did this by aiming low. Best of all, it felt damn good.

Feeling good about myself, I would tell anyone who would listen that I was a runner, and speak proudly of my limited achievements. Sure, I was taking my ego out for a walk and basking in the rays of glory that shone around me.

'I ran 6 km last week,' I told a friend.

'Oh, what was your time for that run?'

'No, I smashed those 6 km over three sessions.'

Delusional? I didn't care. I was going places and feeling good about myself.

Aiming low, I was achieving things many times over, which led to the next inspired idea that unfolded for me. After achieving my goals over and over, I would look at them and wonder: what if I set them just a little bit higher?

And that's what I did. After running twice around the block three times a week, I started venturing beyond the block and running 2 to 3 km a few times a week. I was enjoying the feeling of achieving these new goals, and something cumulative was kicking in. I was creating momentum by aiming low.

Be a loser and win.

Do nothing and go places in your life.

Dream small.

Stop reaching for the stars.

Health magazines never shout these cover story titles, but I was saying these very things to myself and achieving results. I was aiming low and going somewhere with my running.

This led to my waking up one day and sitting on the edge of my bed, thinking about Lance Metz, a few months after meeting

Dad and me.

him. I crossed that fine line of feeling worthless sitting next to him, to being inspired. I was ready. I was ready to climb Mount Everest. I was ready to enter my first ever timed and organised race.

The distance?

'Dad, I'm going to enter a 5 km race!'

'Bravo, my boy. That's so far!'

I found a race online that was in late spring. It was a few weeks away; I was pretty confident that I could prepare for it in time.

'I'm going to run the whole way,' I declared one day to my partner.

'Of course you are!' he said, rather irritated by the obvious statement. 'It's a 5 km *race*, you know?'

That word intimidated me, and indicated that speed may be needed. I'd never covered that distance before, and knew it would be a stretch to run the entire race.

'I am making it a goal to walk none of the race. I'm going to run the whole way, is what I meant.'

His eyes rolled in judgement. That was fine. For me, it was going to be a stretch.

But I needed something more than just telling myself that I was going to run the whole way. I needed a reward, a carrot, something to drive me during the deep pain I knew I was going to feel.

'If I finish the race *and* run the whole way, I'm allowing myself a Big Mac, large Coke and fries!'

His eyes rolled again.

I'm a recovering drug addict. The reward centre of recovering addicts' brains got a lot of attention from us in our using days. Once I'd put down the drugs in recovery, I learnt that reward came more from spiritual sources. Well, some of the time. Not always. I wasn't perfect. After this race, I was going to get myself a gluttonous, addict-friendly, mega-reward!

Race day came, and I was up early, dressed and ready to go – with some nerves, but not too many. *I can do this*, I told myself. But more importantly, I was potentially going to have a Big Mac, large Coke and fries afterwards. I hadn't had much junk food for a few months. I used to eat it at least three times a week in early recovery – I'd reward myself for another day clean and sober with these sweet and tasty words: 'Meal number two with an extra piece and coleslaw, and a 500 ml coke,' at the KFC Drive Thru; 'Big Mac, large Coke and fries,' at McD's; 'Large calamari peri-peri pizza,' at my favourite bistro and pizza joint, Espresso.

That had all landed up on my belly, and I was carrying an extra 10 kg, easily, at that time. I'd managed to cut back for a few months, so this reward at the end of the race was a well overdue treat – one that was enough to get me to the start, with a mission. I was not going to walk a single step of this race!

During the race, I saw way older, more overweight people shuffling all around me. If they could, I could. And I did it with a
Big Mac under my foot with each step I took. Trees turned into
shoelace McDonald's fries. At water points, I imagined large
McDonald's-branded cups overflowing with Coke. The surrounding hills curved like the McDonald's Golden Arches, and
the sky was full of McFlurry clouds. I was going to hammer this
race and reward myself.

'Welcome to McDonald's, how may I take your order?' the
lovely lady said from the speaker at the Drive Thru. This was my
McDonald's moment: the moment I had pushed hard for by running my first-ever 5 km race, and not walking once.

Before we'd got home, the entire meal was finished. Bloated
and burping like a university student after a keg of beer, I retired
to the couch, super happy with my achievement.

I was blown away by the power of the reward I'd decided to
give myself. Lying on the couch, I realised that rewards would
become a central part of my recovery and health journey. Just
like drugs had tickled the reward centre of my brain, this feeling
of accomplishment is what hooked me now – in a different, and
successful, way.

'What if you hadn't run the whole way?' my partner asked that
afternoon. 'What would your punishment be?'

I stared at him. 'Punish myself for walking? Are you crazy?' I
was really taken aback by this punitive thinking. Failure had never
occurred to me – I had aimed low and got a delicious enough
reward – but what would I have done if I hadn't reached my goal?
At that stage, I didn't know. The years ahead would show that
realistic goals and adequate preparation would lead to success,
most of the time.

There were times I'd fall short of a goal. Many times, in fact.

But punishment was not in line with my journey of self-love. Most days were going to be good, and the bad days would be nothing to worry about. Punishment for not attaining something I'd worked hard towards? Penalising myself, while trying to make a better me? That kind of thinking was not going to come near me.

The only way was forwards; even failure was forward movement, in my mind. I had punished myself enough for so many years with alcohol and then drug abuse.

So, 'Let's go get an ice cream,' I said.

Ummphf, ummphf! The music thuds in my ears, electro at 120 beats per minute – Tiësto, the world's greatest DJ, pumping some uplifting trance music. The crowd is full of energy. People everywhere, bumping against each other. Wide smiles and even wider eyes greet me with a nod – an acknowledgement from a total stranger that says we are celebrating this crazy time together in the same way.

'Hey, how are you doing?' A pretty lady in her mid 20s greets me with a huge smile. She's chewing gum and I ask her for some. We are bouncing to the beat and she is next to me – a total stranger, one I add to my collection of instant buddies. *Who is she with? What is she fuelled up on?* I wonder. My body is hot and my palms are sweating, but my bald head is cold. I rub my hands on my head and release the smell of Tiger Balm, that potent smell which gives an added head rush. The kind that many Ecstasy-filled nights are marked by.

The music changes gear and another hot Tiësto track hits us. I clench my jaw with an equal mix of excitement and anxiety. The anxiety always comes up at these times. I start taking deep breaths to bring my heart rate down. I'm bouncing to the beat and I see the dark sky has now turned a little bit lighter. The sun will be coming up soon.

Suddenly, the music stops.

I'm not at a rave. Nor am I at an all-night, drug-filled party. My iPod has just stopped playing. At 5:30 on a cold April morning in 2007, I'm at the start line of the Two Oceans Half Marathon in Cape Town. I check my iPod and see that the battery is actually flat. Damn! My music won't be with me on this race – this, my first ever 21 km run! *I need my music!* I panic. I look to the girl next to me and watch her take an energy bar out of her running belt. *Did I pack mine?* I reach for it, just to check that I have it. *Phew, it's there.*

She smiles at me and says, 'How are you doing?' And, without waiting for an answer, 'Good luck! Have a great race!'

I hear this a hundred times this morning. And thousands of times over the years at the start of all my races. This fleeting greeting culture is supportive and welcoming, and isn't new to me. I remember in the past, at raves, everyone around you would smile at you with a wide grin and ask you how you were doing. Total strangers in tight, shiny tops, chewing gum, staring at you with dilated pupils. At my first rave, it threw me a little, having all these strangers ask me how I was. I was self-conscious about being at my first rave, and I didn't know them – why did they care? Over time, I came to realise that they were just code words to acknowledge one another's presence at the same party, in the same energetic space. But I think it had another purpose: they were actually asking how my trip on the drugs was going. I'm sure it was a way for them to check in and compare whether they'd got better Ecstasy pills from the dealer than I had. The way I nodded back must have given them some indication.

A little smile and a nod, and they probably thought, *Oh, a beginner. He's only taken one pill.* A huge grin and wide eyes: *Oh, good for him. He's on something good.* Biting my lip, with flared nostrils and eyes rolling back: *Damn! Where did this asshole get such good pills? Let's ask him. Who is his dealer?*

Here, now, at the race, everyone is full of the same energy. Smiling, nervous, clenched jaws, lots of bounce in their energy and words. Music, sweat, muscles, but not in the pursuit of an all-night party. Not full of drugs and manufactured sincerity. I am among genuine people who are all here to aim high and improve their lives.

In preparation for the race, I had joined a running club. We used to go for 5 km runs on Saturday mornings, which would sometimes stretch to 8 km. During the week, I would run 5 km a day on most days, on the treadmill. Leading up to the race, I'd started running 10 km races. I was getting used to my legs working again. Each Saturday I would bump into Alecia – an accidental new running club mate. She was one of these advertising exec types who are incredibly hyper, a short, dark-haired girl with a great body, always immaculately dressed in colour-coded gym outfits. She didn't wear much makeup. She was really pretty and in her early 30s.

'Hi, I'm Alecia. Let's run together?' she said, firmly shaking my hand. She'd obviously sized me up quickly and realised we could be of similar fitness or speed. My partner had convinced me to join the running club. He was a very good runner, so he never ran with me – it would be nice to have some company on the run, I thought when I first met her.

I was wrong. You get two types of runners in this world: those who want to talk and run, and those who just want to run. I may be a chatty Greek guy, but as soon as I start running I become less so. Perhaps it's my inability to multitask. Once, I fell on my face, running alone on a flat pavement with no gaps in the concrete, trying to read a street sign. I have a permanent scar above my lip to remind me that, when I run, most of my cerebral faculties shut down. Something I quite like, in fact. It's rather like meditation: when the rhythm of the run hits me, I go into another world.

I like that world, a world where Tiësto would play his Olympic dance music set on my iPod. At the opening ceremony of the 2004 Olympic Games in Athens, he was asked to play an hour-long set as the athletes walked into the stadium. It was a groundbreaking moment having the world's hottest DJ play at such an event, marrying modern music culture with ancient athletic values. This is the world I would escape to when I put on my running shoes.

But not at running club. Alecia would make sure she broke any rhythm I had planned.

'How was your week?' she would ask, with annoyingly genuine interest and a huge smile. 'Did I tell you about my knee?'

I may have struggled to remember her name, but *that* I definitely remembered. It was all she spoke about, this knee of hers that she injured a few months ago. An injury, she told me, that required lots of physio – and discussion, obviously.

'Ice, ice, ice it every day,' she would say. That concept was new to me. Why would somebody need to ice an injury? I never asked her why she did it, for fear that it would start another conversation trajectory that would last another two very long kilometres.

Dear Alecia was always talking about herself and her injury. Her level of self-involvement was so great that it never occurred to her that perhaps I wanted to listen to my music. I'd arrive each week with my iPod, earphones plugged tightly into my ears, but would hardly get to turn it on, as she'd very graciously offer to run with me.

Running next to her, I felt some pains in my shins that were new to me. She convinced me they were shin splints. *Ice, ice, ice*, I thought, and ran off after the session to put some on my legs. It didn't help. I went to the physio, who was not convinced that it was anything serious and said I could keep running. He did mention that I was a little tight behind the knees, and that I may not be ready for a 21 km run just yet.

'Ice, ice, ice it.' Of course – thank you, Alecia! 'I think you should rather train for a few more months before you run a 21,' she said. She knew everything. Her powers included leg-injury diagnosis by mere observation, as well as assessment of readiness for a race – not forgetting advertising strategy for multinational brands and voice projection across large car parks.

I had followed a programme and run a fair number of 10 km races for a few months before the Two Oceans. My partner was happy with my progress, too. Besides, we had already booked the flights and made all the arrangements for our trip to Cape Town.

Sorry, Alecia. Tiësto and my partner had spoken.

The gun fires, and we start the race, not quite as I had planned. With Tiësto silenced by a flat iPod battery, all I have is Alecia's voice in my head. 'Stretch, Costa. Ice, ice, ice.'

No! I have to think of something else – which isn't too hard, as there are thousands of people around me, all shuffling as they do at the crammed start of a race. It takes about 10 minutes for the crowd to spread out, and soon I am jogging lightly, my body warming up nicely. The sun starts to come out and I run the first 2 km with a good rhythm. The Two Oceans starts in a leafy suburb near the University of Cape Town. It is these same roads that, 15 years earlier, I'd driven dangerously drunk, a lost young adult numbing out his world, hiding from who he was.

I start to smile. How wonderfully different things are now.

At about 4 km, the course turns to the right and heads off into the Constantia area. It is here that Alecia starts whispering to me. 'Isn't your knee sore?'

No. Go away, I think, and keep running.

She is right.

All I want to do is finish my first 21 km. So, I step off to the side to stretch. It seems to do the trick, and off I go. About 500 m further on, the pain starts coming back. It now feels like my right knee is locking up. I slow down a lot. That doesn't help either. Worse, my left leg starts feeling the same. The muscles behind my knees are seizing up. I stop to stretch again. I am near the 6 km mark. Ahead of me is Southern Cross Drive, a long 8 km climb that winds through indigenous forests. How am I ever going to do this? I decide to start walking. I am going to finish this race: I did not put up with all those hours of training and spend all this money to drop out of this race. What would I tell Alecia?

When entering a race online, you are asked for your full name. The entry system then obviously pulls your name and prints it on your race number. As a result, a lot of the spectators who line the streets get to shout out your name.

'Go Constantinooos!' I hear people shouting.

What? No one calls me that. Not even Yiayia. And now these *xeni* are using my proper, baptismal name. It takes me a while to realise that my elaborate Greekness, in all its glory, has been printed for all to see and repeat.

But how can they focus on it for long enough to be able read it? It's such a long name. Alas, I am walking most of the time – so they have plenty of time. I am walking so slowly that they can even repeat it to themselves a few times before hollering, 'Go Constantinos!'

Run, Constantinos!

'You walked?' I imagine Alecia's disdain, so I sometimes turn my walk into a bit of a shuffle. As the hill gets steeper, I even manage a little trot. At one stage, I am jogging quite nicely. *Finally, back into my rhythm*, I think.

'Go Constantinos! Go walker!' shouts a woman from the sidelines.

Walker? Shit! She is right. My perceived rhythm is hardly a trot. Embarrassingly, I'm not even walking among runners. I've now fallen to the back of the race pack, among the walkers; worse, I am one of the slower walkers. Constantinos is not jogging up the hill. No! His ego is shattered. He is being called a walker.

A spectator in the forest holds up a placard that says 'Run, Forrest, run!' All I can hear in my head is, *Walk, Constantinos, walk!*

I joined a running club to get here, not a walking club! I think, angrily. The rage sets in, and I try hard to block out the pain and just push up the hill. Eventually, the hill tops out and some nice downhills come. I find a way to walk fast down the hills. I have completed 16 km and can feel the end. I start to worry about the cut-off time. I figure that, at my current pace, I will finish just within it. At 20 km, the pain is no longer bearable and I see a physiotherapy tent on the side of the road. I walk up to it to find a queue. If I wait any longer, I'll miss the cut-off. Alecia! Oh no! I would never hear the end of it.

I hardly know her. I don't even have her phone number. I probably won't go back to the running club, but there she is again. On my mind!

I push on and walk towards the end of the race on the university's main sports fields. I can hear music and crowds. I turn into the grounds and see the finish line about 200 m ahead. But about 30 m in front of me, something catches my eye. It's an adult male, no taller than 4 ft. He is a walker. I notice that he has a severe bow-legged deformity. What shakes me most is that he is ahead of me.

Constantinos is not going to be beaten by a bow-legged,

middle-aged man affected with dwarfism. A surge of energy comes from deep within my ego and I start to sprint. My stupid ego pushes the pain aside and I finish a mere 10 minutes before the cut-off time.

Eat that, Alecia!

Most South African runners dream about running the 89 km Comrades Marathon. The 21 km race was hard on my legs and made me think that too much running at 37 wasn't good for me. I had no history of sport, really, and the only muscle memory I had was from bouncing to trance music at parties.

But I needed a challenge, and wanted to keep fit. I remembered the image of that super-fit guy in a Speedo cross-training on the beach in Durban when I was hungover and smoking, on that morning in the early 90s. I imagined him to be a triathlete at the time. I just knew I had some of him in me. Just a little.

Why not try? Besides, mixing up the running with some swimming and cycling would be better for my body. That is when I first got the idea to start triathlon. There was just one problem: I hadn't swum or ridden a bike since I was 14. The bike was a BMX. The swimming was the bare minimum at school in mandatory PT class. I could swim freestyle, but could only breathe to the one side. I did breaststroke with my head above the water, like an old lady in a shower cap. PT class had been torture. As the slowest in the water, I'd always been ridiculed for my pace and bad form.

These voices would always come up – but my purpose was now about finding a thousand ways to live a better life, and the choice was mine to listen or not. What did they know about me anyway? Where were they now, and why would it not be possible? I mean, I had stopped using crystal meth. Surely I could learn to swim and ride?

Call the dealer, draw cash, drive, cut a line, roll a note, snort, repeat. This had been replaced with swimsuit, cap, goggles, race number, sandals, bike, helmet, sunglasses, pump, water bottle, socks, cycling shoes, spare tyre, bombs, tyre patch kit, energy bar, extra water bottle, towel, watch, running cap, running shoes, T-shirt, running shorts, sunblock, anti-chafing cream, cash for snacks, race belt, safety pins. I was ready to pack it all into my car and head to my first-ever mini-triathlon.

'Can I quickly check that I have everything?' I asked my sister.

'No bloody way! It's the third time you've been through it all. I'm leaving now,' she said, and started the car.

She was visiting from the US and I was so happy to be driven to the race – it allowed me to focus. Time to get my head in the zone. That's what you hear other athletes do, so I did the same. The zone was a very small one, however: a 600 m open-water swim, a 20 km cycle and a 5 km run. I had been training for three months at my local gym. I got a cheap off-road bike and, in the past month, had ramped up my training. I cycled a total of 40 km a week, swam about 2 km a week and ran about 15 km a week at the most. The programme I had come up with was my own, and I relied on a few magazines and websites for what I needed to take with me on the day.

My amazing sister was there with her camera, ready to shoot the entire event. She was becoming my biggest fan and supporter, with encouraging calls and texts throughout my early recovery. On every ninth day of the month, she would be my reminder of another month clean. Her devotion to me was unfailing; today was no different.

We chuckled at the irony of the two Carastavrakis kids at a tri-athlon: two of the least athletic people among all these super-fit, focused athletes. We could out-Zorba them on a dancefloor any day, but this was a different, more difficult, story.

The mass-start swim was a washing machine, which meant I panicked. I decided to relax my nerves by just swimming breast-stroke the entire way, with my head above water so I could see where I was going. Granny style, my swimming cap hardly got water on it. It may as well have been a shower cap. I was one of the last out the water. My sister was standing at the water's edge with a few others, shouting for me to keep moving.

'Gooo Costaaaa!' she squawked at the top of her voice. Greeks are not afraid to be heard, and today my sister was deafening among a quiet crowd of demure South Africans. *Mad Greek woman*, they must have thought. I contemplated stopping to greet her, but this was a race, I told myself. I couldn't afford to lose precious seconds. It wouldn't have made a difference; I was already one of the slowest.

As I got on the bike and headed out, I saw some people run-ning. They had finished the ride and were so far ahead of me that they had already started the run. All I could hear was my supportive sister screaming in her loud voice. This was a race for my new life, and she knew it. She'd always had unconditional love for me and blind faith in me. *How could I not succeed with all this sisterly love in my life?* I thought. It must have been hard for her to watch me being absent from my own life and blind to my own strengths. Gratefully, she was never around during the hard drug days, but it must have been difficult to watch me wast-ing years in an unloving relationship with Ronald, drinking a lot of the time, and often crying to her that I didn't really know my way in life.

Today, with her at my side and screaming in my ears, it would be easy to race to the finish line of life's challenges.

And finish I did. When I crossed the line, she ran up to me

and hugged me tight. We jumped up and down and spun around, locked in an embrace.

'Yaaay! I did it. I did it!'

'You did it, you did it!' she yelled with pride.

There was silence all around, but the Greek siblings didn't care about the spectacle. Like our food, we had our own flavour and colour; perhaps we were not to everyone's taste. But we were never shy about celebrating, especially this.

Swim, 600 m: 30 minutes. Cycle, 20 km: 70 minutes. Run, 5 km: 40 minutes. Almost 2 hours and 20 minutes in total. Sobering, given that the winners managed to do it in under an hour. For them, it was about their times. It was for me, too, but it was also about my time to shine.

In triathlon, the sprint format is about the same distance as the mini-triathlon I had just done, but with a 750 m swim. I managed to do a few of these with Helga, a friend who used to do some running with me. The same Helga who first introduced me to the 12-step programme years ago. And yes, she looks like a Helga: she is a tall, beautiful, blonde woman in her early 40s with a strong voice and incredible charisma. We would go to many running races together in the earlier days and, like me, she transitioned into tri-athlon in an effort to increase the challenge. Racing with her was a huge help. It was always more fun to be a confused amateur with a wacky friend like her. Being together was a little distracting at times, as the conversations would often revolve around men and had nothing to do with the sport or the race ahead.

'OMG, don't look now, but that cutie from the last race with the red is heading over to rack his bike next to us.'

'I heard the guy in the blue won last year. Whoa! Look at how he fills that triathlon suit.'

'I shaved all the hairy Greek off me. Took a few hours and many cuts. Cute, though, don't you think?'

Helga and I were clearly there for more than the sport: we were both single, and heading for body beautiful states in the not too distant future.

Being slow and new at the sport was wonderful. Aiming low, as always, we were just happy to be there to compete. A goal was to do a little better than the last race, but we had many excuses on our side if that wasn't the case. So much can go wrong in a race, and each course can be so different; it's often not easy to compare the times from different races. A general indication is what we were after. Did we feel like our performance had been better than in the previous race? That was our barometer; we would qualitatively assess things for days afterwards, always reminding ourselves that by competing alone we were attaining something that most people in recovery hadn't attained.

We'd done about eight sprint races together in the past year. Each race most often presented two different options: the sprint format and the Olympic-distance triathlon. The latter consisted of a 1 500 m swim, 40 km cycle and 10 km run, and was called 'Olympic-distance' because it was the format that the IOC had decided upon when the sport grew in popularity and was finally included in the Olympic Games in Sydney in 2000.

That distance is one that we regarded with reverence. The thesaurus lists 'otherworldly', 'supernatural' and 'godlike' as synonyms for the word 'Olympian'. The Olympic distance, for us, had a titanic, Everest, colossal meaning; never once did we discuss entering an Olympic-distance race.

One December, we arrived at the last race of the year. The day was particularly gorgeous: not too hot, with a clear, blue, Johannesburg summer sky. The race was in Germiston, not too far from central Johannesburg, in a man-made lake with a partial street closure. We had done the shorter course a few times before, and arrived pretty confident about the day ahead. Most importantly, we were in a great mood.

The camaraderie between us was electric. Before registering for the race, I looked at Helga and asked, 'What if we just tried the Olympic today? I mean, we know the course.'

Helga's eyes widened with glee. She must have been thinking the same thing. 'We can take it really slowly,' she said. 'And we can wait for each other, and keep each other company.'

That sealed it for us. The sprint and Olympic fields started at the same time. Should we want to drop out for any reason, we could also just join the shorter race ourselves. The official time and result were not what we were after. As we stood looking at the swimming course – two 750 m laps – we confirmed to each other that we would start at the back and just take it slowly.

The leaders lapped us on our first lap. But we weren't fazed. Getting out of the water almost last, we high-fived each other and headed for our bikes. Time for a small snack and a chat to see how we were feeling.

'This is very doable. We can do this!' I said to her.

'Of course!' was her enthusiastic reply. Snack gobbled and chat over, we continued our 'race'.

Helga was just the kind of tri mate one wanted – she was always ready for a challenge, and didn't take herself too seriously. We were both approaching the middle of our lives and she was also part of a 12-step programme. She'd come down a similar path in her pursuit of health. Being friends from our old drinking days, we now shared many new – healthy – bonds; this Olympic effort would be the newest.

'Oh my God, it's hot – and I'm bloody thirsty,' I said. We were on the last 5 km of the run. The cycle had gone quite well. Helga was a little slower than me, so we took longer than I thought we would. But that didn't matter. We had each other for company and motivation. It was approaching midday, and was turning out to be a scorcher of a day. We hadn't had enough to drink on the bike – we weren't expecting to ride 40 km, so we'd only brought one bottle each. We'd drank a little in the transition zone, but now, well into the run, we were tired and thirsty.

'Where is the water station now?' Helga asked.

'It was here on the last lap, I'm sure of it,' I answered, very confused.

'They must have finished all the water. Damn! Let's look for a race official.'

Those were the last words we said to each other in that race. We both had our caps on, and pulled them down low. We didn't look up while we were running, and just shuffled through the last kilometres. We'd only lift our heads to look for the markers, and saw pretty much nothing else. We just kept on going. No water, no race officials. But we wanted to finish, and pressed on.

The last marker came up, and we knew we were almost home. That feeling when you turn off the road into the sports club's grounds to cross the timing mat and finish was almost upon us. We had almost made it! What a relief! *What an achievement*, I thought.

But something was wrong. Things were a little quiet. There was none of the usual blasting music, and no commentator to spur us on. Strange.

'What the hell? Who died?' said Helga, with her trademark dark humour. She was right. The party was over, and very few people were left behind.

We turned into the sports club and saw the finishing straight.

At these events, there is always an inflatable finishing arch over the timing mat with the sponsors' names on it – a perfect spot for the race photographer to take a picture of us finishing, holding hands high in the air, together. Running underneath the arch was going to be a challenge today, however: it was busy being deflated, and the timing mat had already been rolled up. A lopsided arch in its final stages of deflation stood before us.

We both screamed at the top of our lungs. 'Waaait! Waaaaait!'

The race had ended, and the organisers were packing up. It was game over for the day. With no timing mat, we had one remaining rite of passage that we were not going to miss. You don't just walk off a course and head for your car. You *have* to pass under the inflatable arch!

'Pleeease wait!'

No one heard us. We had 50 m ahead of us, and now it was a sprint to the finish, a race to get under the arch before it hit the ground.

After a full, hot morning of exercise, with too little water and not much nutrition, we had to dig deep. It was us vs gravity, the force that was pulling the arch down. We made it just in time. We had to duck to get under the arch, but we made it!

'Yaaay! We did it! We did it!' we shouted, jumping around in an embrace.

Maybe the photographer was busy taking pics? I thought. What a great photo this would make. Was there anything for us to drink at the end? Any chance of a finisher's medal, or a goodie bag? Any chance of being included in the finishers' list, with no timing mat? No one could answer us, as there were no officials around. The day had ended, the race had been wrapped up and the prizes had all been handed out while we'd still been out somewhere on the run.

Two triathlon souls. The very last to finish a race. But we finished.

CREDIT: GARETH JACOBS

*'And me, I still believe in paradise. But now at least I know
it's not some place you can look for,
'cause it's not where you go. It's how you feel
for a moment in your life when you're a part of
something, and if you find that moment …
it lasts forever …'*

— RICHARD, *THE BEACH*

EPILOGUE

There was once a 12-year-old boy and he hanged himself.
A LETTER TO HIM:

Dear Costa

You are not what other people call you or say you are. Don't listen.

Your bullies will grow up to be small men. They will fear your inner strength one day.

Tell someone what you are feeling. Your family loves you.

Wear whatever goddamn necklace you want to.

Barbie-and-Ken is not the only way to pair up in life.

You are gay. It's okay.

Next time you feel a tic coming on, turn it into a dance.

ABBA have broken up. Horrible, I know. But there will be ABBA compilations, Broadway shows, movies and soundtracks for the rest of your life.

Breathe! Madonna is coming.
And Gaga, Cher, Wham!, Boy George, Strictly Ballroom and Patrick Swayze in *Dirty Dancing*.

Step away from the sparkling wine at Alan's bar mitzvah next weekend.

Slow down. Running from life doesn't sort anything out.

Miss Greece won't win a Miss Universe (until at least 2019) but Eurovision 2005 will go Greek.

Boys cry.

If you feel like running, run a little more. You have some Olympian in you.

Don't try everything once. Some things are, indeed, bad for you.

You only live once. Read that again. Slowly.

If someone makes you choose them over your family and friends, they don't love you.

Yiayia knows. She also sometimes doesn't know!

God loves you. Just figure out who He really is for you.

Celebrate being Greek. Baklava over Bundt cake *always*.

You are incapable of working at a large corporation, no matter how much you charm your interviewers or yourself.

One day life will be so different that you'll visit Greece holding your boyfriend's hand in public, wearing a jade Buddha around your neck. You will be a vegetarian. They will still have something to say. Absolutely none of it will bother you, though.

Being raped becomes part of your journey. That's okay. It will teach you acceptance, resilience, forgiveness and how to fight back.

It's called weed for a reason.

Aim low!

Nancy Reagan was right. Just say no!

Feeling shame for who you are is like adding too much salt to tzatziki – it destroys everything.

There may be ups, there may be downs, but there will always be Miss Universe.

Demi-Leigh Nel-Peters will win Miss Universe for South Africa for the first time since you were 8 years old, and it will happen while you are writing your book. A sign from above? You bet!

Start spreading the news ... in 2011, you will complete your first marathon in New York City in under four-and-a-half hours.

Be yourself. Accept yourself. For you, it's a matter of life and death.

ACKNOWLEDGEMENTS

I would like to thank Sarah Bullen and Kate Emmerson of The Writing Room for refusing to write my book for me and making me sit down and do it myself.

Thank you to the whole team at Bookstorm for believing in me and helping my story come to life.

Thank you to my family, friends, colleagues, therapists, coaches, and eyebrow ladies. I am who I am because of your love.

I would love to hear from you. Kindly email me at costa@ thisiscosta.com.

If drug and alcohol addiction is affecting you or someone you love, contact the South African National Council on Alcoholism and Drug Dependence (SANCA), and visit www. sancanational.info for more information. I am neither affiliated nor qualified to recommend treatment options, but you can access many resources through Google.

For more information on me and the talks I do, please visit my website at www.thisiscosta.com.